Deep Breaths

"Michelle is an inspiration to millennial moms everywhere! Her realistic, raw, and simple approach to navigating live as a millennial mom is not to be ignored. She is wise beyond her years and is a true inspiration of what healthy motherhood should and could be!"

Jordan Page
YouTube Vlogger

"Michelle is what the millennial mom strives to be. She has such a positive outlook on life and enjoys each moment with her family in such a real and raw way. Sharing wisdom and experience with a touch of style and class, Michelle is a role model to so many of this generation!"

Jeannie Brattrud
YouTube Vlogger

"Reading Michelle's journey as both a mom and a millennial woman, with hopes and admirations of her own, I couldn't help but feel like I was sitting down to coffee with a close friend, sharing some of our hardest and most beautiful struggles. Michelle's depiction of both the blessings and the challenges that every millennial mom faces, is raw, refreshing, and shows truly how unique the millennial generation is. Sharing her high moments, as well as the low- you get an intimate look into her life as both a young woman and also a mom who is passionate about everything she does. Millennials have both the advantage and the curse of social media, and Michelle so candidly speaks life and hope into a generation of moms who just want someone to tell them they're doing it "right".

Jaimie Kight
YouTube Vlogger

"Michelle's passion for helping other women navigate the highs and lows of motherhood in this modern age is a gift to all who come in contact with her. Her genuine and sincere personality made this a joy to read, and feel like you have an instant friend in your own mom tribe!"

Alycia Crowley
Blogger

"Mchelle is going to help ease the worries so many new moms have and inspire them to be the best version of themselves."

Jennika Anderson
YouTube Vlogger

"Not only does Michelle touch on the accuracy of what it means to be a millennial, but really speaks for what generational mothers are feeling in today's society. As a young, millennial mom myself, I was able to connect on so many levels."

Brittany Sills
YouTube Vlogger

Deep Breaths

THE
NEW MOM'S HANDBOOK
TO YOUR
BABY'S FIRST YEAR

Michelle Pearson
PARENTING VLOGGER

Cover Design: Laura Mejía
Layout & Design: Laura Mejía

For permission requests, please contact the publisher at:
Mango Publishing Group
2850 Douglas Road, 3rd Floor
Coral Gables, FL 33134 USA
info@mango.bz

For special orders, quantity sales, course adoptions and corporate sales, please email the publisher at sales@mango.bz. For trade and wholesale sales, please contact Ingram Publisher Services at customer.service@ingramcontent.com or +1.800.509.4887.

Deep Breaths: The New Mom's Handbook to Your Baby's First Year

Library of Congress Cataloging-in-Publication has been applied for.
ISBN: (paperback) 978-1-63353-643-2, (ebook) 978-1-63353-644-9
BISAC category code 2017909206

Printed in the United States of America

Dedicated to:

My incredible best friend and soul mate Brad Pearson. Your love and support gives me all of the strength that I need to get through this crazy life. I love you and I am honored to be your wife.

My children Will, Max, Molly, Abigail and Margaret. For teaching me what unconditional love is. I am forever grateful for your laughs, cuddles, and smiles. Thank you for shaping me into the mother and woman I am today. I love you all more than you could ever imagine.

Table of Contents

FOREWORD

By Amanda Mulherin

've known Michelle for a few years now, in fact, I like to think we're part of the O.G. Mom's on YouTube. If you're one of the older millennials (like me *cough* O.G. stands for original gangsters) basically we've been making videos about babies and all that motherhood entails for a seemingly long time.

I discovered Michelle while I was still living in Malaysia. We both make videos about beauty, motherhood and life, and we hit it off right away! I like to think of my piece of the internet as a safe spot for women to land. Those Mom's working their way through motherhood and life, and want a friend to share coffee with or just to share. Michelle was that friend for me. A smile that lights up a room. A message that resonates with positivity and love, that conveys a delicate vulnerability which is motherhood. Thank goodness for this era of technology that allows us to lean into our screens and connect with like-minded creators near us and around the world.

Being a mother is tough work. In this time of technology, mothers can be quickly judged if they share too much online, everyone has an opinion and is more than happy to tell you how to parent. Don't even get me started on self-diagnosing illnesses thanks to a few online questionnaires! In my experience, having a voice and sharing your story online has only brought amazing things to my life and those around me. Being able to document your journey in motherhood, find a community of people sharing their stories and feel connected to women around the earth is what it's all about. They say it takes a village, and being able to create one online is incredible. Motherhood can be lonely and what we see others doing online doesn't always resonate with our experiences, it can leave us feeling isolated and lost. Michelle has always been so open and honest in her parenting journey. From her struggles with pregnancy weight gain, her joy and pride in building a large family, to her journey through postpartum depression, Michelle has lent her voice to those walking a similar path.

Is everyone watching motherhood videos on YouTube? No. Although if you ask me, they should be! I'm so grateful to the internet for bringing me (and you!) to Michelle. In writing this book, and sharing her story through these pages, Michelle extends her community reach to those mothers in need of a friend. Whether I'm making a day in the life vlog, having fun over live video with my viewers or speaking on stage about women and mothers in digital media, my message is always the same; we're all in this together, and sharing the highs and lows is what makes motherhood such a delicious time. From one gangster momma to another, Michelle I support you, I love the work you do and hopefully one day we'll actually get to meet in person. Until then, I'll see you in your next YouTube video, in our village.

INTRODUCTION

Why Millennial Moms Are Different
Than Any Other Generation

will never forget the day we found out. The test was positive and we were ecstatic. We were pregnant! I was 26 years old at the time and my husband was 23. We couldn't wait to take a picture of the test and share it someday soon with our family and friends via text and social media.

I remember hearing that it was not socially acceptable to announce your pregnancy until you were out of your first trimester. This proved difficult, as I worked side by side with my mother and sister every single day. I wanted to follow what I was told, because what if I had a miscarriage? I did not want to go against what I had heard. Nonetheless I gave in. The smells and the bustling Thai restaurant that my family owned proved to be a difficult place for a pregnant woman in her first trimester. I had to tell my family. So I did. Before I was 12 weeks along. I somehow felt like a rebel of sorts.

The moment we posted on Facebook and Instagram that we were pregnant, the congrats and "you need to's" started coming our way. I remember feeling extremely overwhelmed. I was told that I HAD to read "What to Expect When

You're Expecting." Oh, and I just HAD to stay away from fish, deli meats, and soda. Of course, I was extremely excited to finally be a mother too. And I was excited to meet my baby boy. But oh, how I felt the need to do what I was told by lots of those around me for fear that I was not doing it correctly or that I wouldn't fit in.

On Sunday, October 24, 2010, we welcomed William Peter Pearson to our family. Labor was perfect. He was perfect. I, on the other hand, was swollen and about 70 pounds overweight.

I still laugh when I look at my pictures from that day. I felt so small because I no longer had my child inside poking my ribs all day. I could lie on my stomach again. But I was still so far away from how I looked nine months before.

Once Will was born, my husband and I announced it to the world via our cell phones. We were so excited to FaceTime our relatives who lived in different states. I remember my phone blowing up with notifications from old friends, long ago ex-boyfriends, and current acquaintances. We were in heaven and were so excited to share our baby boy with the world.

I remember asking the doctor to be checked out a day early from the hospital. My husband and I were anxious to get home and start living our lives as parents. We couldn't wait to figure the whole parenting thing out.

Within a few weeks, I learned how little I knew about motherhood. Of course, I figured out changing a diaper quickly and how to bathe my little Will. I was thankful that nursing clicked for us. I cherished those moments rocking him on our soft microfiber rocker. I remember not being able to stay awake during the night feedings, so I would turn on YouTube videos to keep myself awake and alert. Not only was I providing nutrition for my baby, but I was learning about how to apply eyeshadow too!

As a first-time mom, I didn't know what was normal for a baby to do. Sure, I had been given a laundry list of books to peruse, but who had time to read all of that? It wasn't until Will was a few weeks old that I started getting the questions from family and friends. "Is he sleeping through the night? How many naps does he take during the day? How long does he sleep when he sleeps?" I started feeling self-conscious. Will wasn't the greatest sleeper. No, he wasn't going all night without waking up. If he woke up, my instinct was to rush to his side and pick him up, and then if he wanted I would nurse him back to sleep. It was then that I realized how different my parenting style already was from others'.

When I told people he wasn't sleeping well or that I would nurse on demand, I started to get suggestions such as, "Why don't you let him just cry it out? Have you read '**Babywise**'? You HAVE to read that book. It works for every baby." So began my journey with trying to get my baby to be the perfect sleeper by the time he was 6 weeks old. (As a mom of three currently pregnant with baby #4 and baby #5, I laugh at this now.)

I tried it all. I bought as many books as I could find on Amazon. I read online articles and I talked with friends. I wanted so badly to be able to give the answer "yes" when asked if he slept through the night. Guess what? Nothing worked. Nothing. I felt like a failure. Why am I telling you this story? Is it to make you feel sorry for me as a first time mom? Well, yes. Kind of.

No, I tell you this so you know where I'm coming from. I'm not a scholar. I'm not a pediatrician. I am just a millennial mom of three (soon to be five) kids. Everything I share in this book is what I have learned in my last 6 years of parenting. I share it because I want you to know where I came from and how I came to the conclusions that I have. Let's continue on, shall we?

Social Media Pressures

Millennial moms are different than any other generation simply because of social media. We are told on a daily basis how we should look, what we should buy, and what is good or bad for our children. Some struggle with infertility and have to watch friends and family post all over their Facebook that they are expecting. While it is so wonderful to have an instant connection with those we love most, it can also be painful for many.

According to BabyCenter.com, 53 percent of moms feel overwhelmed trying to create the perfect life for their children. I know that a lot of that pressure comes from social media and the perfect life people like to post. Instagram layouts

My Notes

are all color-coordinated or have a theme.

Babies happily play in their leather moccasins and harem pants. Moms with their perfectly braided hair pose in front of the Eiffel Tower on their family vacation, all while they carry their designer diaper bag. All so very beautiful, but not necessarily realistic or obtainable for everyone.

There have also been multiple studies that have shown how social media use can cause depression in those who use it often. Individuals are bombarded by acquaintances who are traveling to faraway places, getting graduate degrees, and building the home of their dreams. It is no wonder that people feel upset with the way their life has turned out. "Comparison is the thief of joy" is one of my favorite quotes of all time. The problem with social media is that it is the link, it is the carrier of depression in many ways. It makes people feel inadequate or that they are not enough because they are not stacking up to those they see online.

I cannot lie. I gain a lot of weight when I am pregnant. No matter how much I exercise or how much I try to control my diet, I pack on the pounds. Social media for me during pregnancy is torture. Not only am I surrounded by peoples' "perfect" lives, I am also constantly shown through my newsfeed pictures other girls who are pregnant but hardly look like they have gained a pound. I know all of us have different bodies and different genetics. But when I see a pregnant woman with a six-pack, it is hard to not let myself feel bad about the weight I have put on.

For some reason the millennial generation feels the need to try to appear happy and perfect at all times. While I feel it is wonderful to be hopeful and optimistic, I find that only showing that side can be harmful to many. People need to know that we not only laugh, we also cry; that we celebrate when something fabulous happens but that we also mourn too. Honesty and transparency have always been an important thing to me on social media, and I can only hope that I can spread that to other millennials.

There's An Online Cure For Everything

Millennial moms are also different because of the access we have to information. If our child wakes up with a fever, we have options. Sure, we can call the doctor or the nurse's advice hotline, but why not check out WebMD, google, and text 15 of our closest friends first?

I cannot tell you how many times I personally or my friends have been able to diagnose ourselves or our children with something without consulting our doctors. Of course, I always try to get the final say from a REAL doctor, but for some reason I always find peace of mind figuring it out myself. Online. On my phone. It just feels good.

After I had my third baby (my first girl!), I was feeling extremely hopeless. We had just moved to a new house, new neighborhood and started a new life. I was buried in work, staying up late editing and brainstorming YouTube video ideas. I would find myself crying for no reason at all. I knew I had everything I ever wanted. A hot husband who worked hard and was good with kids. My dream house was finally a reality. I had two handsome, smart little boys and an adorable chubby baby girl. But I was so sad. What once brought me joy (running, training for triathlons, making YouTube videos) no longer brought me happiness. I knew something was wrong but couldn't put my finger on it.

I didn't figure it out until one night when I was on Facebook and saw an article pop up. I can't remember the title verbatim, but it was something to the effect of, "How to know if you suffer from postpartum depression." I clicked on it, thinking, "Why not?" As I skimmed the article and found a checklist of symptoms, I realized that I was answering "yes" to every question. Thanks to this online article, I had been able to diagnose myself with postpartum depression.

After I realized why I was feeling the way I was, I immediately felt better. There was a reason I was feeling the way I was. There was a problem, and I could find a solution. I was not crazy. I can't tell you how happy that made me. I called up my therapist, made an appointment, and got better within a few months' time.

While I was lucky to manage to diagnose myself by learning and reading online, it can also be comical what mothers and fathers can find. I have myself entered my symptoms into WebMD or Google and have self diagnosed with serious chronic diseases and other terrible ailments. I find this most entertaining at times.

Working Mothers

Millennial moms are different than any other generation, simply because more women are working than ever in recorded history. Not only are more women getting an education, but many stay-at-home mothers are becoming "work-at-home mothers" too.

I grew up in a biracial home. My father was American, while my mother was born and raised in Thailand. I was taught my entire life to work hard and to dream big. My parents are both workhorses and instilled those same values in my siblings and I from a very young age. I distinctly remember my mother asking my three siblings and me on multiple occasions, "What kind of doctor are you going to be?" My brother would say "Cardiologist!" and my sister would say, "Dermatologist!" I remember hating math and science, so I knew I could never go that route, but I knew I wanted to be the best at whatever I ended up choosing. I knew that I wanted to be a working mom. Fast forward to many years later. I wanted to pursue broadcast journalism. My senior year of college I was able to do an internship at the local CBS affiliate in my city. While it was fascinating knowing the latest about what was going on in the world, I found myself sad when I heard the lead anchor say, "My nanny sees my children more than I do."

After that, I was a bit confused. How could I pursue my dream job as broadcaster but rarely see my children? I knew that somehow everything would work out and turn out how it was supposed to.

When we had our first child, I decided to stay at home and be with my son full time. I knew that somehow I could be the mother I wanted to be while pursuing my dream of being on camera. I just wasn't quite sure how that would happen just yet.

Then after just a few months of being a stay-at-home mom, I found YouTube, and the rest is history. For the last five and a half years, I have been lucky enough to be a work-at-home mom. It's no easy task, but we make it work. I don't have dedicated office hours or a boss to report to. But I do stay up late (as I am doing right now as I write this) to get my job done. Sometimes I check my email too often at the park because I know I have a deadline coming up. I squeeze in conference calls at nap time and send in proposals in the Target parking lot. I love being a social media influencer and mother all the same. I live in Utah, the land of MLMs. If you don't know what that means, you obviously haven't been to Utah.

The majority of people in Utah are very religious, and that means that traditional family roles are practiced a lot. Many women choose to stay home but want to find something to keep them busy or help bring in a little side income. To a lot of them, this is accomplished by the means of some sort of product.

I cannot even count on my two hands how many times I have been offered leggings, jewelry, Norwex

My Notes

cleaning towels, or essential oils to buy. While I feel it is wonderful to be able to do those things from home, I can definitely say that it is too highly saturated in the area that I live. I am proud of the women I see doing it because they are pursuing their work to better their lives and the lives of their family members.

I can't speak for all mothers who work outside of the home because I have never been one. I can say that I know that everyone has their reasoning, and I more than respect that. There are more women than ever in the workplace, and I love hearing what they are achieving. I can only imagine the joy and pride they feel to be able to handle both work life and family life.

Every Millennial Mom Is An Influencer

In 2014, business.com had their Influence Central Consumer Insights team study the millennial market. What they found out was:

Millennial Moms lived their lives "steeped in technology and social media", and 95% of them owned a smartphone! Millennial Moms loved online reviews when it came to shopping and getting the right products for themselves or for their family.

Millennial moms also LOVE to share their experiences. "They have a very powerful need to share their experiences and pass these insights on

– with 90 percent of Moms posting reviews often/
occasionally. In fact, Millennial Moms – more
so than Millennials – use social media to share
insights and expertise."

And finally:

Millennial Moms use social media to:

- Be an influencer (86%)
- Express opinions (83%)
- Connect with the community (79%)
- Give advice to others (72%)
- Make brand recommendations (71%)
- Share stories with others (70%)

I cannot tell you how many times I have posted a
picture of myself, my family or my home, and then
one of my subscribers, friends, or neighbors has
left a comment asking me where something in the
picture was from.

I also cannot tell you how many times one of my
friends has posted a great find or a sale that was
happening. I also am a little embarrassed to admit
how many times I have seen the post, hopped in
my minivan, and headed straight to said store to
get the very same deal. More times than not (to my
husband's horror), it has been online and so much
easier to make my purchase.

There is something magical about being able to
share something you love with others and feel
like somehow you are helping them. It means
something to have your opinion validated and your
taste respected.

My Notes

When I started my YouTube channel five and a half years ago I wanted to do just that. I wanted to help mothers out there realize that what they were feeling was not crazy and that they were not alone. I also wanted to influence them for the good. I wanted them to believe that they could be successful mothers amidst all of the chaos of our day and age.

I personally look to other mothers who are influencers for a variety of reasons, whether it's for fashion inspiration, home decor ideas, or just to get myself excited to work out. Women are a powerful influence on one another, and thanks to social media, Millennial Moms are able to do that now more than any other generation.

A couple of years ago I got stuck on the tarmac at an obscure airport in the Midwest. I was in the plane for 6 hours straight. Thankfully, I had my iPad, and I had just downloaded a book by Stephanie Nielson called, "Heaven is Here." I read the ENTIRE book while I waited for my plane to get fixed. I laughed and I cried. I felt motivated and inspired. I finished the book and promised myself that I would be a better wife and mother and that I would never take my health or my life for granted again.

Stephanie Nielson was in a horrific plane accident 8 years ago. Over 80% of her body was badly burned. Her blog and other social media have become very popular among Millennial Moms, and she has shared her story with people from all over the world. She shares messages of hope and peace. She loves being a mother, and that enthusiasm is contagious. She has indeed influenced others for good.

Millennial Moms Are Open

I am a person who believes that everything happens for a reason, the good and the bad. I believe we are meant to have those experiences so that we can share them and help uplift others who may go through something similar.

Thankfully, I am a Millennial Mom, and we are more open than any other generation. Whether it is infertility, postpartum depression, or a miscarriage, women in this day and age are more willing to share their experiences in hopes that they can help others who may be feeling the same pain. What once was taboo to discuss is no longer. Anything can be talked about in this open-minded generation.

There are Facebook groups for anything you can imagine. There is support for any topic or trial. Mothers in this generation need not feel defeated or alone.

I have found that my most popular YouTube videos have been those in which I have opened up about something personal. The comment section is always flooded with viewers saying, "I'm so glad I'm not alone!" and, "Thank you for being so open. You have helped me."

While it can be great that women are more open in our time it can also be a bad thing. Sometimes too much information can be shared online, and things can get awkward quickly. Whether it's one person complaining about children pooping or another leaving an obscure status update, sometimes too much is too much. Of course, to each her own, but I have never been a fan of the naked kids in the bath picture or those showing too much skin. Others feel it is their prerogative to post pictures multiple times a day. Sometimes too much is just too much.

Millennial Mom Relationships

The dynamic of mom friends has changed dramatically in this generation. Because of social media, women no longer have the need to pick up the phone and catch up with a friend. Women do not have to see each other as often, because they feel like they see each other daily on their social media newsfeed.

While it is fabulous to have an instantaneous connection with friends from the present and past, it can definitely hurt relationships. Instead of going to lunch and catching up, lots of millennial moms simply "like" a picture or write a quick comment. What once was long conversations on the phone or at the park has turned into quick text message threads.

My Notes

While women in this generation have never been so intertwined and connected, they have never felt so alone at the same time. Relationships feel like they don't need as much work because of the quick day-to-day interaction via social media. Many times I have found myself talking to multiple friends via text and/or slack but feeling so unfulfilled and distant. We all need human interaction. Especially when the only other humans we see all day are speaking about things like Pokémon and Shopkins.

So there you have it! Some of the many reasons why Millennial Moms are different than any previous generation. While we are lucky to have all of the wonderful connections that modern day life gives us, we are also faced with challenges that our mothers and grandmothers never had to face.

CHAPTER ONE

How To Become The Mom
You Want To Be

Like most things, success as a mother comes after trial and error. No single person is born with all of the experience and knowledge to be the "perfect mom." Unfortunately, most of us forget this simple concept as we become mothers and enter into this stage of life.

It is no secret to those who know me that I love to sing. I would like to believe that I came out of the womb singing. I remember as a child longing to be a famous pop star. My mom would tell me that the best place to practice was in the shower because of the echo. Every time I shower to this day I always serenade my husband and children. As I entered high school, I fell in love with the theater. I loved acting and being someone else in front of a crowd. I loved feeling the emotions of the characters I was pretending to be. Musical theater was a combination of two of my favorite things. Imagine my excitement when my high school decided to do "West Side Story" for that year's musical.

I began taking singing lessons from Dayna S., the sweetest woman. She was kind and patient and made me believe that I could be the best classical singer there ever was. My lessons with her went overtime almost every time. We would get carried away with a song or technique. I was drunk on classical singing. After months and months of rehearsing with Dayna, I felt completely competent and ready to get the lead role of Maria.

I remember the day that the cast list was hung up on the theater room's door. A crowd assembled around it as everyone looked for their name and found out what part they were going to play. Imagine my horror as my name was nowhere to be seen anywhere on the top half of the sheet. I was given the character of "Teresita." No lines, no need for a mic, nothing I had prepared for.

Despite not getting the lead role, I decided to stick with it and be a part of the musical anyway. We spent months rehearsing for that musical. It was one of the best times of my life. We grew close as a cast, and my love for music and theater grew even more. What felt like a disappointment initially became a distant memory as we closed the curtains on the final performance.

My love of theater and music never changed. I realized that even though I had worked hard for months and months to prepare, I still wasn't as ready as the girl who got the lead role. She had been studying classical music for years and had a voice like an angel. Just because she got the role didn't mean that I couldn't sing. It didn't mean that I couldn't love or embrace music because I didn't have the spotlight on me. Instead, it made me work harder. Over time I became better, and my love for music and singing are still a part of me today.

Why am I telling you this silly experience from my high school thespian days? I am telling you because in a lot of ways it reminds me of how I felt as a young mother. I had read book after book, talked to many friends, and educated myself as much as I possibly could on the subject of pregnancy and motherhood. When the time came, I wasn't ready. I wasn't perfect. I didn't know it all, even though I had worked hard to find out as much as I could. In the end, it didn't matter. Because with each day, with each child, I have learned more and more about myself and what type of mother I dream of being. Motherhood takes work. There is always going to be someone who has been doing it longer or who does it better than us. That doesn't mean we aren't good mothers. That doesn't mean our work to do our best is done in vain. The key to becoming the mothers we want to be is by following the simple steps I talk about in this chapter.

Taking Care Of Yourself

I truly believe that first and foremost we need to take care of ourselves. You know when you get on an airplane, and they tell you that in case of an emergency if the oxygen masks fall, you must first put on your mask and then help the person next

to you. YOU have to save yourself FIRST. Then you can save others.

The same principle applies in motherhood. How can you guide your children in their daily struggles if you yourself can hardly keep it together? How can you teach your children about love and happiness if you do not feel it in your own life? You must first know and then you can teach.

There are myriad ways that we can take care of ourselves. I personally believe (in a non-insulting respectful way) that every woman would benefit greatly from a therapist or counselor at some point in her life.

As women, our minds race a million miles per minute. We always play out worst-case scenarios in our heads. We panic when things don't go according to plan. There are times we may think everyone hates us or is out to get us. Of course, these are broad generalizations, but I think it's safe to say that most of us have felt these feelings at some point in our lives.

I never saw a therapist until I was pregnant with my third child. My boys were still young, only two and four years old, and we decided it would be a great idea to move from our home to a rent free situation at my parent's old home that I grew up in. In order to do that, we had to do some remodeling and cleaning out of my childhood home to make room for our little family of five. We spent months and months driving back and forth so we could paint, clear out the basement, and be there while flooring guys came and went. We also didn't want to sell our previous home using a real estate agent. We wanted to keep the money ourselves. This meant keeping our house in tip-top shape so it could be ready to be shown to an interested buyer at any given moment.

I remember feeling so overwhelmed. We were moving away from our close friends and Brad's job. My parents both worked 90+ hours a week, so I knew they wouldn't be able to help us much once my baby daughter came. My anxiety levels had never been so high.

My husband and I spoke about finding a therapist, and we found one named Heather. I am forever grateful to her because she honestly changed my life. She allowed me to bring my boys into her office while we had our sessions. She never forced me to keep my sessions exactly in the allotted time. She made me feel comfortable. She validated my fears

My Notes

and feelings. She gave me tools I could use to deal with relationship stresses and pain that I had experienced and never fully gotten over.

There was something magical about being able to be completely open with someone. It was wonderful to know that someone was listening and that they understood why I felt the way I did. I knew immediately I had to share what I had learned with those around me. I felt so much freedom. I felt like a new woman.

Taking care of our minds is important, but so is taking care of our bodies. Exercise is proven to help our bodies produce more endorphins and therefore makes us happier. Some find exercise works best when they work out with friends and so are being held accountable. Some women love Zumba, CrossFit, or swimming. For me, running changed everything. I could go on long runs that helped my mind escape the stress and pressure I was under. It also gave me a sense of identity separate from my role as "just a mom." I began setting goals for myself. Not only did it help me feel a sense of accomplishment, but I was able to shape my body into a healthy one. Running changed my body and mind. For my 30th birthday, I decided to gift myself a present of running a half marathon. I trained for it for months, and I cried as I crossed the finish line. All of my hard work had paid off, and I achieved something I had always longed to do. I daydream about long runs now that I'm pregnant with twins. I get winded just walking up my stairs. Someday I will wake up as the sun comes up, and I will put on my running shoes and head to the trail near my home. I will blast my Britney Spears Spotify playlist and run my mom worries away. Someday I will push my body and mind and run faster, longer, and harder than ever before. Until then, I will just patiently wait.

Finding Your Mama Tribe

Let it be known that 90% of my life I have been an outsider. I have always found it difficult to fit in or to find many other girls or women who felt the same way I did about life. I recognized this at an early age. My parents uprooted our family of six from Salt Lake City, Utah, to Ta'if, Saudi Arabia, when I was four years old. We lived there until I was 11 years old, and my memories of those years are very clear.

We were one of only a couple of Christian families in the area and the local school. I remember being mocked at recess by children who told me I was going to hell because I didn't believe in the Muslim religion.

When we finally moved back to the United States in the early 90's, I was extremely excited to finally feel "American." I remembered instantly feeling like an outsider. I didn't know what a nickel, dime, or quarter were worth. I spoke with a slight accent, one that I had picked up from the children at the international school I had attended in the Middle East. My mom was from Bangkok, Thailand, and my dad was American. I was the only biracial kid in any of my classes. Kids made fun of the food we ate or the way we dressed or talked. I hadn't

seen any of the movies the kids talked about at recess or visited any of the places where they vacationed. I remember wanting so badly to fit in. It was rough.

For some reason fitting in during any time of our lives feels good. It feels wonderful to be accepted and cared about. Most importantly, it feels good to belong.

As a new mother, finding a mama tribe is key. It is imperative to find other women who are in the thick of it with you. Some may have older kids and others might have only one. It is good for the soul to be able to complain about last night's lack of sleep or how tired you are trying to juggle work and motherhood.

How does one find a mama tribe? I can definitely tell you from personal experience that it is no easy task. It takes a lot of guts and a thick skin. It takes determination and a desire to make an effort outside of your relationship with your husband and children.

When my husband and I bought our first home in 2011, we were so excited to finally live in a place of permanence. We wanted to live there for a minimum of five years. I so desperately wanted to feel like a part of the community there.

I wanted to have friends, and I wanted my two little boys to be able to have play dates and feel comfortable in the area. I took matters into my own hands and started a playgroup and a joy school in the neighborhood. It was so wonderful to have one day a week to look forward to. We would

My Notes

go on outings to the aquarium, park, or just to the McDonald's play place. It was so great to feel social again. We also had a joy school that we set up. Each week one mom would prepare a lesson for the half a dozen three year olds. They didn't pay a whole lot of attention, but it felt good that we were at least socializing the kids. At least we were giving it our best shot.

One thing that I learned in that neighborhood, however, was that not everyone was interested in having mommy relationships like I was. Some probably thought I was too much into always organizing activities, etc. To be honest, I cried a lot back then. I just didn't understand why other moms like me would want to be alone at home with their children all day, every day. I remember another mother telling me once that people didn't like me because I was "too motivated." Social relationships were key for my survival as a stay-at-home mom. I needed the interaction to help me get through those long, exhausting days.

Finding friends as a mother is tough stuff. Some of us may live in big cities where there aren't a lot of families. Others might live in tiny towns where the population is under 100. If I can give you any advice it would be to never give up. Be creative in how you search for friends. Be brave, and don't be afraid of rejection. I promise you it will happen. You will get burned and you will not be invited to dinners or girls' nights. It will be okay though. I promise. Because in your quest to find friendship, you will find yourself. You will be able to recognize who you like to be around and who is worth being around.

The fabulous thing about being a millennial mom is that we have options. We are no longer tied down to just our little town, city, or home that we live in. We have the internet. We can communicate with women from all over the world within seconds. That is such a powerful thing. I receive emails and messages daily from women from other continents and places that I will probably never see in my lifetime. They share with me their fears, triumphs, and family stats. They tell me about their children and their children's accomplishments. They tell me things they've never told anyone before. All because they feel like they can confide in me. Some because they say they don't know anyone else who is a mother at this stage in life.

There are so many ways online to find your mama tribe. I have found many through YouTube, and I know there are countless forums and Facebook groups for moms of all backgrounds. I currently belong to one specifically for Mormon Moms of Multiples. I read fascinating things on that group every single day. I learn about tips and tricks on how to potty-train twins or how to deal with the end of a twin pregnancy. It makes me happy to know that I am not alone in any given situation.

Two years ago I had a strong feeling we should move our family into a different neighborhood. It confused my husband initially, because we had planned to be in our first home for a minimum of five years and it had only been three. After lots of talking and discussing our options, we decided to build a new home in the new neighborhood.

This new neighborhood has been my saving grace in so many ways. There are young families everywhere. We have a park, tennis court, and swimming pool. There are 20 kids in the neighborhood who are my oldest son's age. There are young families who are in the same stage of life as us. It has been a dream for so many reasons.

The greatest reason has been that I have finally found my mama tribe. I have found women who stepped up and helped me the way a family member would. I have experienced so much of this kindness, especially since becoming pregnant with my twins. There have been days where I haven't left my bed for hours on end. Countless members of my tribe have taken my children, brought dinner, and contacted me daily to support and uplift me.

I am not naive, and I know that this perfect mama tribe situation does not exist everywhere. That doesn't mean that we can't create our own support system wherever we may be. I have found that in order to receive kindness, we have to dish it out too. We have to serve and look for ways to help other moms out there. I believe in karma, and I know that if we are kind and serve others, more often than not we will receive that kindness in return.

Look online for playgroups. Start one in your area if you can. If you go to a playground or zoo and see a young mom like yourself, strike up a conversation. Some people might be rude or disinterested, but others will be looking for friendship just like you. Having that support system is key in becoming the mother you want to be. It will help give you courage when you feel weak, and it will uplift and inspire you to become more than you are.

Finding Your Passions In Life

I know it might seem like a distant memory, but before you had children you were a person. You had interests, maybe a job of some sort, and maybe a great social life. You were probably passionate about something, whether it was your job, school, traveling, or fashion. The key to being the mother you want to be is remembering those passions once you actually become a parent.

Far too often we get so busy changing diapers, giving baths, and feeding our little ones that we forget who we once were. Of course, being a mother is a gift from God. We are so lucky for the opportunity. It does not mean, however, that we are supposed to disappear and change everything we once were before our babies came.

Life with children is hectic. There's always something going on. For me it's soccer practice, homework and errands. This is all on top of the diaper changing, morning sickness, and anxiety I feel about a certain situation with a certain friend who doesn't talk to me anymore.

Of course we can be passionate about motherhood. I happen to be VERY passionate about the topic. It's actually the reason why I started my YouTube channel almost six years ago.

I do think that too often we put ourselves and our interests in last place. We lose ourselves and who we once were. In some ways, this is a good thing. But in other ways it hinders our growth and happiness.

I have actually found a lot of new interests since becoming a mom. Because of my busy mom schedule, I can't necessarily entertain all of my interests the way I used to. I have found my love for running and my love of talking to people on the internet. They are both therapeutic, but they also are now part of my identity.

I encourage you, young mother, to try something new. Ask a friend to join you. If you don't like it, try something else. You will find something you love. I know you will. It is wonderful, exhilarating, and exciting to be passionate about something. It gives you something to work towards and something to be proud of. I have found that nine times out of ten when I have fallen in love with a new hobby or interest, I have helped encourage other moms to follow suit. Enthusiasm is catching, and when you find a hobby or something you love, others will try doing the same.

I also love having my own hobbies and interests, because it forces me to make time for myself. Because of my job as a YouTuber, I have to film in a quiet space by myself. I also have to edit and answer emails, all things that force me to take time out and be alone. My house is usually chaotic, with neighbor friends running in and out. Sometimes it feels like I don't even have doors on my house because so many people come and go. Don't get me wrong, I love it more than anything, but it makes it difficult sometimes to find peace and quiet.

My Notes

These moments are crucial so I can be alone with my thoughts.

Life is too short not to find something you love. Do something for yourself once in a while. Make yourself happy. Being a mother is an incredible thing, but that doesn't mean that it is the only thing you are. You were once a fully functioning person before you had babies, and you will have to be a functioning person again once all of your babies are out of the nest. Find your passion in life. Find what you love to do and what makes you happy. These are all steps on the path to how you can become the mother and person you want to be.

CHAPTER TWO

The Good, The Bad, The Ugly

The interesting thing about motherhood is that you never fully enter a stage where you feel like you have it all together. There is always growth, and there is always constant change in our lives and in the lives of our children.

The fabulous thing too is that we are not the first ones to mess up as mothers or wish that we had known more after the fact. Thankfully, there have been women before us who we can learn from and take note of what mistakes were made.

The role of mother has evolved a lot over time. While most women in the 1960's were stay-at-home moms, now 70% of women work outside of the home. Thanks to modern medicine, women who once were not able to conceive can, with the help of fertility drugs, and become the mother they have always wanted to be.

Motherhood is one long learning process. There is always a new situation to be handled and new products to try. Do not be discouraged by all of the unknowns. Look to women from your past and present and learn from them.

My mother is from Bangkok, Thailand, and moved to the United States when she was 24 years old. She met my father soon after, and they were married in 1980. My parents had four children, my brother being the oldest, me being the second child, and then two other sisters following me. Raising children in a biracial home (my father is American) was no easy task for my mother. She was constantly trying to find a balance between what she had always known and what she wanted to change since she now lived in a different country.

If I have learned anything as a mother, it is that adaptation is key. My mother taught me this in many ways. She is an incredible cook and her Thai dishes are the best I have ever tried. She is gifted. Since we were living in Utah, she learned to cook more Americanized meals as well. We appreciated this; American food to us was a special thing. To most kids, mashed potatoes, pot roast, and casseroles were what they grew up on. I, on the other hand, had Pad Thai, som tum, and massaman curry as my go-to dishes growing up.

My mother was also stricter than my father and most American moms out there. As my siblings and I grew older, she grew to become a lot more comfortable with the way American teenagers acted and loved being involved with our social activities and events. Adaptation was key to her happiness as a mother in a completely different culture.

I feel like it's also important to remember to always have balance as a mother. Try to not be too much of one thing. I have found that putting too much pressure on yourself and your children to be too perfect or too clean can affect everyone in a negative light. My mother found a perfect balance between what she had learned in a Buddhist culture and what she was living in as a mother to American children. She always taught us her family history and spoke to us in Thai. I will be forever grateful to her for teaching me the language as it has helped me learn multiple languages since. I love that she found a balance of incorporating her heritage into our family without completely forgetting the other heritage we had from my father's side of the family.

It is important to remember that as a mother we are always being watched by our children. They are constantly watching how we react, what we say, and how we handle certain situations or people.

My mother is not perfect, and neither am I. I am grateful for her being vulnerable enough to show me that as a young girl. She always expressed her feelings openly, and I am grateful for her example that it is okay to cry, and that she showed me that it is okay to not always have on a perfect smile. She would make mistakes as a mother as well. She would get upset with us, but she would always apologize for whatever she did wrong, teaching us that she was figuring it all out just like we were.

My mother also taught me and made me believe that I was the greatest thing to ever happen to this world. She believed in me and always threw compliments my way. She would ask my siblings and I what kind of doctor we wanted to be when we grew up. She would tell us how important education was and that if we worked hard we could achieve anything we wanted to. She not only drilled this into our minds, she supported us full throttle as well. When I decided I wanted to be a thespian, she signed me up for classical voice lessons right away. She signed me up for piano lessons when I was four and supported all of my dreams, no matter how random or silly they might have been.

She not only told us that we were all amazing, incredible human beings with great potential, but she showed us how to work hard and how to get there. She always had a business of some sort that she was starting. Whether it was a custom wedding dress business or selling her paintings, she worked hard to find success by using her talents. After my siblings and I all left the house, she fulfilled her lifelong dream of owning her

My Notes

own Thai restaurant. It has now been open for ten years, and it is one of the most well-known Thai restaurants in the valley. Famous celebrities like Olympian athlete Apolo Anton Ohno or American Idol finalist David Archuleta have been seen in her restaurant many times. She takes pride in her food and in the fact that she can help provide an income for many families that have parents who work in her restaurant. It has been incredible to see my mother reach the success she has always dreamed of because she worked hard to get there.

I have heard the saying that what you say to your children becomes the voice inside their head. I believe this to be true more than anything. What we say to our children, how we make them feel, dictates what they say to themselves throughout their lives. If we tell them they are loved, they are capable, they are talented, and they are important, they will grow up believing and knowing that. I think that is one of the most powerful gifts that you can give to your child, to help them see that they have the potential to be an incredible human being.

Children need confidence, and I am forever grateful to my mother for instilling that confidence in me. There have been numbers of times throughout my life when I have been the outcast, and others have told me that I am not amazing and that I am not talented and that I didn't deserve friendship or success. Thankfully, I have a mother who loves and believes in me. I am eternally grateful to her for instilling the confidence in me that I can be more than what others may try to make me be.

As I have three children currently and two on the way, I think often about what I can personally do as a mother to help my children reach their greatest potential. I know that if we are good examples, if we instill confidence in them, and if we try our best to balance our lives and adapt, we can achieve that goal.

My father's mother, Clista, was the perfect grandmother. She made homemade raspberry jam, baked the best sugar cookies, and knew how to keep a home in order. She always had cookies in the cookie jar, and I can still remember her pink bathroom and the way it smelled. She was kind, worked hard, and made a career out of being a stay-at-home mom. She attended all of my basketball games and musical performances. She was the best cheerleader. She and my grandpa would take out each grandchild individually on our birthdays. We could choose wherever we wanted to eat. It was always such a special treat for me to get that alone time and one-on-one attention from my grandparents. They made me feel special and loved.

One of the greatest things that I learned from my grandma Clista was that family was important, and that no matter what we may have going on, it is important to make children feel loved. It was important to her to always give us that special one-on-one attention.

I have tried to implement that in my life as a mother. It doesn't happen as much as I would like, but I enjoy trying to have one-on-one "dates" with my children. I let them choose where they want to go grab a bite to eat or some sort of treat.

Sometimes it's ice cream, sometimes it's Wendy's, or perhaps a donut at a grocery store. Then we sit and chat. Many times I have been brought to tears during these little dates because I realize how much I miss being able to give them all of my attention all of the time. I learn so much about each child and what is important to them. It has been so wonderful for my relationship with each one of them.

One of the things that scares me as a young mother is that what I teach my children now or how I treat them in the present will not be enough as they grow older, that somehow I'll miss something, and then when they are faced with a certain problem, they won't know how to handle it because I forgot or missed out on teaching them. Mom guilt is very real in my daily life.

As mothers, I think it is important to remember to try not to care too much about being "perfect" and going "by the book." There are a lot of people telling young mothers what we should be doing and how we should be doing it. They tell us that if we do not do it their way, then we are failing or we are not good parents. It is most important to go with your mommy gut. Yes, it is important to teach your children manners, values, and how to keep themselves safe. I think it is also important is to teach them how to be confident, how to care for others, and how to adapt in certain situations. Being a parent is not a math equation. If you do A and B, it will not ALWAYS equal C. And that is okay. We will be okay, and so will our children if we don't go exactly by the book.

I'm thankful to my parents for always showing me how imperfect they were. They showed my brother, my two sisters, and me their weaknesses. As a 32 year old mom of three (soon to be five), I appreciate this now more than ever. I saw my parents struggle with normal things that parents do: money, jobs, each other, children, etc. I saw them struggle, but I also saw them rise. I saw them work through it. It taught me that with perseverance and hard work I could accomplish anything I set out to do. They taught me it was okay to be human, to be upset sometimes. They always made me feel validated and they listened when I told them my problems and concerns. While my mom and dad were my parents, they were also my best friends.

I often refer to my children as my "best friends." Of course I am their parent, but I want them to be honest and open with me always, just like my parents wanted me to be with them. I find that it is so crucial for parents and children to have that close relationship. I could literally tell my parents everything without fear of judgement. I remember in middle school my dad always telling me that if I was ever anywhere that I didn't feel comfortable, no matter what time of day or night, he would come get me. I called him multiple times when I ended up somewhere where there was underage drinking, smoking, or even marijuana use. He never got upset with me for being in those situations, and that made me want to never do those things. I felt so close to my parents that I never wanted to ruin that trust or the relationship that we had.

My Notes

Even though my oldest is only six, I try all of the time to get him and my other children to talk to me. Not just simple conversations about what they learned in school that day, but how they felt, how they think someone else felt, what made them happy, what the best part of their day was. If they make a mistake or if I know they are being dishonest, I ask them to apologize and to tell me the truth. I tell them I will be more upset with them for lying than I would be about the actual mistake. I want my children to do something because THEY make the right choice, not because I force them too.

The key to good parenting is learning from our own and others' mistakes. We have friends, parents, grandparents, etc. to teach us what to do and what not to do as parents. I often remember as a child saying to myself, "When

I'm a parent, I will never do that." It think it's important that we make an effort to remember what we didn't like when we were children. It's important to look to our parents' mistakes and fix them and make them better for our children.

Our parents, grandparents, and those before us were not perfect beings, just like we are not perfect. The most important thing is that we are trying. We will fail, but we will also prevail. Our children will be like us; they will remember the good, the bad, and the ugly. But they will also remember that we tried our hardest to be the best parents that we could be in our given circumstances.

So don't give up, my friends. Keep going. Make a conscious effort each morning to listen more to your children and be more attentive to their needs. Make changes when necessary and know that your children will love you regardless of how perfect or imperfect you are.

CHAPTER THREE

Embracing, Finding, Defining
The Mother Within

One of the first things I realized as a new mother was that I needed to decide what type of mother I wanted to be. Did I want to be a working mom? Did I want to be the mom that followed the Cry It Out method? Did I want to be strict on sleep schedules?

I am almost positive that you have asked yourself some of these same questions. I promise you that as your children grow and develop you will have to ask yourself these questions with each new stage. Do you want to be the cool, go with the flow mom? Do you want to let your kids ride the bus, or will you drive them on your own? Do you want your kids to be more into sports, or will you have them choose more artsy activities?

The beautiful thing about motherhood is that you can always change who you are. You do not have to define yourself as a young mom and stay that way throughout each stage of your child's life. As mothers, we grow with our children.

The crucial part is defining the mother that we want to someday be. When we are aware of that,

then we can take the necessary steps to reach that goal.

In this chapter I want you to explore different scenarios and answer different questions about different types of motherhood. There are no right or wrong answers. My goal is to help you understand more of who you are and who you want to be as a new mom.

These questions do not have right or wrong answers. They are meant to help you explore these topics and maybe give you ideas of how to handle each situation.

In this first section, I want you to embrace the mother and person that you are. I recall doing this exercise with my therapist a couple of years ago. Initially it felt very uncomfortable. I realized how little I gave myself credit for. Do not be shy.

Now, maybe that was harder than you thought it would be. Am I right? I find that as women and mothers, we far too often spend time talking negatively to ourselves about what we should be and what is wrong with us. I hope this exercise made you realize that you do have positive qualities and that you are good enough. Far too often we are too harsh on ourselves and are our own worst critics. That inner voice that speaks to us all day is rarely saying positive things that uplift us and make us happier.

When my therapist asked me to write positive traits down about myself, I thought of maybe 10 different things. When I came back to her with my list, she laughed at me. She then went

Exercise #1:

Write down 10 good things about yourself.

-
-
-
-
-
-
-
-
-
-

Good job! Now that you've written 10, write 25 more. Don't be shy. Nobody is going to see this except you.

-
-
-
-
-
-
-
-
-
-
-
-

Exercise #2:

Now that you have listed positive qualities about yourself, I am going to ask you to do something a little uncomfortable. Talk to your spouse, your mom, or your best friend. Ask them to write down a list of wonderful qualities that you have. Write those down here.

off and listed dozens and dozens of positive qualities that I had. I realized in that moment how little I appreciated who I was and what I had accomplished in life. It was such a good reminder to me that I needed to be less harsh and less critical of the person that I was.

On those days when it seems that all is lost and that you are not enough, I encourage you to look back on these two lists. It is a healthy reminder of who you are and who you are capable of being.

Now that you have answered the previous questions, it's time to take a second and think about the answers you gave. Are you spending enough time with yourself? Are you making time for your partner? Are you making time for socializing? Other questions tell you more about what is most important to you as a new mother. Once again, there is no right or wrong answer to any of the above questions. I hope that answering those has helped you think about motherhood as more than just being a mom.

As a new mom six years ago, I would have been stumped by a couple of those questions. I was rarely seeing friends and never took time to myself. I was confused about what kind of mother I wanted to be, because everyone told me different versions of what they thought was the "perfect mom."

In this last section, I want to focus on goals. I find it is most important as a mother to set goals for yourself every day, every week, every month, and every year. Goals help give us a sense of purpose beyond just the duties that come along

Exercise #3:

Exploring the type of mother that you want
to be.

Now that we know and are familiar with
some good characteristics that you have,
it's time to explore what type of mother you
are. Answer the questions below:

#1: It's your child's first birthday. How are
you going to celebrate?

#2: You've had a stressful week. Baby is sick, you're only sleeping one hour a night, and you have been overwhelmed with your part-time job. Your husband offers to take the baby for a couple hours one night. What do you choose to do?

#3: What is the state of your home? Is it perfectly clean? Dirty?

#4: What is your favorite thing about motherhood?

#5: How often do you and your husband go on a date with each other?

#6: What is the one thing that you want your kids to learn from you?

#7: How do you plan on disciplining your children?

#8: What is one thing you will never do to your children as a mom?

#9: What is your go-to dinner?

#10: How often do you take time for yourself?

#11: How often do you socialize with friends, family, or neighbors?

#12: What is one thing you want your children to remember about you?

#13: When do you feel the happiest?

#14: What are your favorite hobbies?

#15: Who is your mommy mentor and why?

----

with motherhood. Goals remind us to take care of ourselves on an ongoing basis.

Three years ago I decided that one of my main goals was to participate in a triathlon. I had never been on a road bike, but I loved to swim and run. I had my two boys (three years and one year old) at the time. I wanted to lose my baby weight, but I also wanted to prove to myself that I could do anything I put my mind to even though I had two children. I spent six days a week working out. Once my baby was down for bed at 8 p.m., I would get my running shoes on and hit the road running. I would spend nights at the local swimming pool swimming laps. Sometimes when my husband came home at 5 p.m., I would hop on my bike and go on a 15 mile bike ride. It was challenging, and I had never before pushed myself so much when it came to physical activity. I didn't care about my time or if I beat anyone. I wanted to prove to myself that I could do it. I also wanted to show my followers on social media that a woman could take care of herself while taking care of her family.

I'll never forget the feeling that I felt when I finished that triathlon. I crossed the finish line with my arms raised up high in celebration and tears in my eyes. I was proud of myself. I had worked tirelessly for months for that single moment. I promised myself that I would always take time to take care of my physical and mental health.

Am I saying that every mom needs to do a triathlon in order to feel accomplished? Definitely not. Goals can be simple, but they can also be complex. One thing I enjoy doing is filling out my planner each day. I write down the goals that I have for the following day. This helps keep my mind clear and organized. It helps me feel less stressed and overwhelmed. One of my favorite things to do (as nerdy as it sounds) is to check off these goals on my list. Some days my goals might be as simple as 'fold laundry' or 'vacuum.' Other days are more complicated, like 'change oil', 'cook dinner for a friend', or 'film a video.'

Just like daily goals, long term goals feel so good to accomplish. They of course take longer, but the sense of accomplishment is great. I encourage you to set goals that take you outside of your comfort zone. Look for goals that will help you meet people and that involve your talents. Accomplishing goals is a journey that helps you find yourself and in turn helps you figure out what type of mother you are.

Now that you have written down multiple goals, go through each of them and decide what you need to do or change in your life in order to make that goal happen. Do you need to hire a babysitter more often? Do you need to join a fitness club or Facebook group?

Motherhood is a long, challenging journey for many, but it can be enjoyable too. It can be rewarding if we figure out who we are and who we want to become. I encourage you to check back on these exercises often in order to check in with yourself. Taking care of ourselves helps us become the mothers and women we desire to be.

Exercise #4:

- Write down 3 goals for tomorrow.

  -

  -

  -

- Write down 3 goals for the week.

-

-

-

- Write down 5 goals for the month.

-

-

-

-

-

Write down 10 goals for the year.

CHAPTER FOUR

Delicate Balance

I am sure you have heard that women are great at multitasking. Something in our brains is wired to be able to have a million different thoughts running through our head at any given moment. I am so grateful for this, because motherhood is all about balance.

I want you to step back for a second and think of the busiest you have ever been in your life. Were you juggling a failing relationship and studying for a final while trying to work your part-time job and attend college classes? Were you running on 2 hours of sleep because you went out dancing the night before? I remember those days very well. I remember being exhausted beyond measure, but I always knew that at some point I would catch up and be able to get a good long nap in at some point of the process.

Sadly, I feel as though motherhood has felt like that same thing, only multiplied by the last six years of my life, and I have never officially "caught up." Of course I am not saying that anyone who is not a parent is not tired or exhausted or stretched beyond themselves, but adding children to the mix creates an entirely different element that I did not know was possible.

Children are exhausting. Being pregnant is exhausting, for lack of a better word. As you find in this book, the key to making it out to the other side is to find balance in all things. Balance in relationships, balance in "me" time, and of course if you're working, balance in work and family life.

Some of you might be reading this and you have just had your first child or you're preparing to have your third. I believe every stage is important, but it is important always to remember that you can achieve everything your heart desires if you find balance.

Work-At-Home Moms

When my first baby, Will, was born, I was not working at the time. My husband had one month left of college, and the economy had just crashed. There were not many job opportunities at the time, and while we were nervous about our financial situation, I knew that staying home with my baby was what I needed to do for him and for myself at the time.

After my husband graduated, he was lucky to find a job. It didn't pay us a lot, but we were grateful because the job market was so poor. We were thankful to his grandfather for letting us live in his basement apartment in Salt Lake City. It was dark, but it was big, and I was so grateful to have room to raise my little son in.

That first year was very lonely for me in that basement. I didn't know anyone in the area, and I was still figuring out the entire motherhood world that I had just entered. We didn't have lots of extra spending money, so I couldn't go shopping or take my son to expensive children's museums, etc. I was bored.

My son would nap multiple times a day, and since we didn't have money for cable, I spent hours and hours watching videos on YouTube. Back then the only videos to be found were beauty videos or funny cat videos. I realized there wasn't any content for mothers out there.

Far too often I found myself googling things like, "How to get your baby to sleep through the night," or "What baby products do I need for the first year?" It was then that I decided to put my broadcast journalism degree to use and start talking to the camera again.

YouTube became not only a hobby but a passion for me. I found myself connecting with mothers from all over the world. They would tell me that they felt just as inadequate as I did, and that I wasn't alone in my fears or struggles.

I didn't know how to monetize my videos on YouTube, but after a while I started making a little money here and there. Some companies even started sending me products for free. I realized that my little hobby/passion could also be a nice little side income as well. I remember being excited by my first check for $100. Even though it wasn't a ton of money, it was still something, and I was able to do it all from home.

Fast forward to five and a half years later; I feel so blessed to be able to work from home. I feel like I get the best of both worlds. I can earn an income to help support my family, but I can also be here for my kids as they come home from school and need my attention.

As clichéd as it may sound, I feel like I am living my dream for that very reason. I get to do everything I love. With that, though, comes a price. I have found myself stressed beyond measure because I can never fully separate myself from my job or from my family. This makes it difficult to focus on lots of my tasks.

There are more mothers than ever who currently are work-at-home moms. Social media and the internet have made it easier for mothers to share their talents in ways they have never been able to before. Income can be made simply from having a popular Instagram account or from selling your art on Etsy. Lots of women are also photographers or cooking bloggers. It's a wonderful time to be able to pursue your dreams and also be able to do it all from the comfort of your own home.

Working at home has its positive aspects, like not having to pay for daycare and so forth, but it also has a lot of drawbacks as well. As I stated above, it has been difficult for me in the past to separate work and family. It wasn't until I decided to make my own office space that I felt like I could do that.

If you are a work-at-home mom, here are some of my tips on how you can find that perfect balance.

---

1. Find your own space.

I actually got rid of my laptop and got a desktop computer and placed it in my office. That way I could only do my work in my office. This helped me focus and stay concentrated. I could also close my office doors, and everyone in the family knew that meant that mommy was working.

2. Make your own office hours.

Since your schedule is somewhat flexible, give yourself specific times of the day or night when you will work. That way you will be more productive in a smaller amount of time, but you will also be able to stay on top of your work and not feel overwhelmed trying to get all of your work done on the same day.

3. Get help when you need it.

If you find yourself drowning in work, find a way to get help. Whether it's an assistant or a babysitter once a week, find a way to get help from outside sources. Your brain, heart, and body will thank you.

4. Put your phone away.

If you're anything like me, you are on your phone way too much for work. This can take away the attention that your kids need when you are with them. I try to put my phone upstairs in my bedroom while I hang out downstairs in the family area with my children. That way my notifications, emails, messages, etc. can wait for another time when I'm not spending quality time with my children.

5. Don't put too much on your plate.

Business is important, but business is not THE most important thing. Be okay with turning down deals or offers. Know that if it's too stressful for you to balance everything it's okay to say no to job opportunities or social obligations.

Maternity Leave

Although I have never taken maternity leave, I know many women who have. It is not something I pretend to know a lot about, but I do know, love, and respect women who are doing what they need to do in order to make their family and work lives work for them.

Maybe you are reading this book while you are currently on maternity leave. Maybe you're reading this thinking, "How does this lady even know what it feels like to be me? To have to leave my young baby and head back into the workplace?" Well, the honest truth is I don't know what it feels like. But my heart goes out to you.

I know some women go back to work because they have to help make ends meet. I know others who are fulfilling lifelong dreams and wanting to continue in their careers. That is the beauty of life. We are all different and we all have different circumstances. It's how we can all learn from one another.

My advice to you if you are a woman who has been on maternity leave or if you're going to be on maternity leave is to be open about it. Help those around you understand your circumstances. Help other women learn about what you are going through.

Maternity leave for most women is only a matter of weeks. You have a short amount of time to figure out the whole motherhood thing, and then right when you start to get a feel for it someone else has to take over.

My advice to you, dear working moms, is to seek balance when you can. All things in moderation when possible. Of course, demanding careers can make it difficult, but when you can turn off your emails and enjoy being away from work, do it.

I find in many cases that working moms handle juggling and balancing in such a graceful way. Since their time at home and with their kids is limited, they are great at multitasking and being efficient with the amount of time that they do have.

Postpartum Depression

According to the Centers for Disease Control, approximately 600,000 women suffer from postpartum depression each year in the United States. I remember hearing a statistic like that during my first couple of pregnancies, but it didn't mean much to me at the time. It wasn't until I had my third baby that postpartum depression affected me too.

There are lots of reasons why women experience postpartum depression. Some women get it more severely than others, and some women get it soon after they give birth, while others might not have it until months later.

Before I dive into my personal experience with postpartum depression, I wanted to give you a few signs to look for. I find that far too often the mother's mental health is not taken care of as well as the infant's health. Most doctor appointments are for the baby, and most of the time (depending on your OBGYN) the mother's appointments are more about physical things healing and not necessarily about the mother's mental state.

Depression can creep up on you, and many women do not even realize it. Here are some of the signs of postpartum depression to look out for, according to the Mayo Clinic:

- Depressed mood or severe mood swings
- Excessive crying
- Difficulty bonding with your baby
- Withdrawing from family and friends
- Loss of appetite or eating much more than usual
- Inability to sleep (insomnia) or sleeping too much
- Overwhelming fatigue or loss of energy
- Reduced interest and pleasure in activities you used to enjoy
- Intense irritability and anger
- Fear that you're not a good mother
- Feelings of worthlessness, shame, guilt or inadequacy
- Diminished ability to think clearly, concentrate or make decisions
- Severe anxiety and panic attacks
- Thoughts of harming yourself or your baby
- Recurrent thoughts of death or suicide

You may only have some of these symptoms, but you don't need to have all of them in order to be suffering from postpartum depression.

If you feel like you are dealing with PPD, it's very important to seek help immediately. Talk to your doctor, partner, family, and friends, and let them know what is going on. No mother should have to suffer in silence.

As I've mentioned earlier in this book, I have suffered from postpartum depression myself. I have actually dealt with just regular depression too, so you would think that it would be easier to recognize it when I had it

After I had my third baby, I was beyond overwhelmed. I was working a lot, getting little sleep, and had little time to myself. I felt like I was drowning and that I couldn't gain control of any aspect of my life. I was living in a picture-perfect neighborhood with lots of

My Notes

friends, kids, and social activities. My husband had a great job and my kids were happy. We had just built a new home, and everything on the outside seemed like it was perfect. I technically didn't have anything to be sad or depressed about. It wasn't until one day when I saw an article pop up somewhere online that talked about postpartum depression that I went through the checklist and realized that I had it.

Realizing that I had PPD was a big step for me. Finally there was a reason for feeling the way that I was feeling. I wasn't crazy. It was hormonal, and there wasn't anything I could have done differently to not have it. It was not my fault. Such a relief to recognize what was wrong so I could then be proactive and do what I needed to do to take care of myself so I could take care of my family.

After I figured out what was really going on with me, I shared it with everyone I knew, my close friends, my family, and my social media following. I wanted it to no longer be a taboo subject. I was literally contacted by hundreds of women who told me they had also suffered from PPD. Many of them suffered in silence because they were ashamed and embarrassed. I also wanted those close to me to understand that I had distanced myself for a reason and not because I was upset or offended by anything they had done.

Being open about PPD may not be for everyone, but I found that it worked wonders for me. I found support from friends and family members. Most of them had suffered from it themselves and were able to give me the love and advice that I needed at that time.

I realized that my life had become completely out of balance. Since I wasn't getting the rest or "me time" that I needed, I was not getting a chance to rejuvenate. Then I was so tired that I became completely withdrawn from social situations, which made me feel lonelier than ever.

Thankfully, with the help of a therapist, my amazing husband, good friends, and family I was able to get over PPD. It was not an easy road, but it was worth it for myself and for my family. Finding happiness as a mother is definitely all about balance, balancing work with family time, friends, and "me" time. It takes extra effort and work, but anything that is worth it always does.

CHAPTER FIVE

A Day In The Life of
a Millennial Mom

Before we start, I want to write a small love letter to my personal assistant. To all the personal assistants that mothers need. Because being a millennial mom takes the old adage of 'it takes a village' and amplifies it in a world where there is less time than ever. It doesn't simply take a village anymore, now it takes a village and their smartphones. Phones, phones, and more phones. A millennial mom is not a millennial mom without one. We wake up and check our phones. We get ready and we use our phones as a DJ, a calendar, a teacher, and so much more. We check Facebook, Instagram, and Snapchat as we connect with our families and friends. We (I hope it's not just me) check our email and social media multiple times a day. When we are out and about with our kids, in traffic, or at the store, we hand them our phone for the parental version of: Netflix and chill. Before bed we check our phone again to see what tomorrow has in store. In the year 2017, our phones are our personal assistants, our guides, our everything.

Social media is the number one thing that differentiates Millennial Moms from any earlier generation. Multiple times a day a mother in this

generation is connected to thousands of people. She might post pictures of her baby's first steps or check on friends who live on the other side of the country. Some moms even follow women they don't know personally in an attempt to continue to learn on this journey. It is easy to forget that these bloggers, YouTubers, and influencers are real people, people who are facing similar highs and lows that you deal with. Beauty bloggers, bakers, DIY experts, they all make up your social network and so in a strange way, they all know you and help you on your pregnancy and new motherhood journey.

If a Millennial Mom doesn't know how to do something, she can find out how at the drop of a hat. She can find recipes, tips on how to lose the last of the baby weight, or the steps needed to sew a pillow. Information is everywhere.

With all of the information and the capability to see what so many other people are doing, it's difficult for women in this day and age not to feel overwhelmed.

In this chapter I want to give you my tips on all the things that Millennial Moms deal with. As a woman who spends way too much time on social media and on my phone, I can assure you I have experience with what works and what doesn't work.

Mom Guilt

One saying that sticks out for me immediately when we talk about mom guilt is the following:

"Behind every great kid is a mom who's pretty sure she's screwing up."

Mom guilt is real my friends. Because we have access to so many other women out in the world, it is hard to not compare. But the worst mom award goes to me, because I have never ever in my 6 years of parenting done 'Elf on the Shelf.' I have seen plastered all over social media the incredibly creative naughty things that the Elf is capable of. I'm always so impressed by the moms' commitment to thinking of something new and exciting each and every day. I also am the worst mom because when I'm sick, my kids watch way too much Netflix. Sometimes my kids tell me I'm on my phone too much. I have had YouTube followers tell me that I don't feed my kids healthy food and that my kids aren't properly fastened in their car seats. I wish I had time to have good quality time with each of my children, but the days aren't long enough and sometimes I just want to have a minute to myself. The list could go on for the entire length of this book.

I know I'm not perfect. I never will be. And guess what? Neither will you. And guess what else? That is okay. We are human, and the fact that we even feel guilty is I think a good sign that we probably aren't as bad as we think we are.

I know that it is difficult as a young mom to look at other moms who seem to have it all together. Social media, as you know, does not help us with this. We only get a tiny glimpse into someone's life. Their 10 seconds of perfection for the picture. In all reality, we all feel that we lack in some aspect of motherhood. Trust me, I have met so many moms throughout my life, and the ones who seem to have it the most together still struggle a lot with feeling adequate and feeling like they are doing enough.

Here are some of my tips on how you can combat those feelings of inadequacy and guilt.

---

1. Limit your time on social media. Every day, put your phone in your bedroom, office, or laundry room. Let it sit in there untouched for a couple of hours.

2. The second you find yourself feeling guilty about something, stop. Think of three things that you do well as a mother instead.

3. If there is something specific that you feel guilty about, accept it, but then move on. No use wasting time on something that is already over and done with.

4. Take a look at what you can change to make yourself feel better about your situation.

5. Find joy in the simple things. Make a list of three things every night that brought you joy throughout your day. Look for the positive in your life.

Me Time

One of the things that mothers need to do more is to have ME TIME. Too often we are pulled in 10 different directions at any given moment. Someone is always needing us to help them, to guide them, to direct them in the right direction. Motherhood is full of social pressures, and too often mothers don't take the time they need to refuel.

My Notes

My first three children did not take milk in bottles. Let me repeat that for emphasis. THEY DID NOT TAKE BOTTLES! Do you know what that meant? It meant I could never leave them for the first months of their lives. If I did leave, I was paranoid that they would become hungry, so I never went anywhere for a long period of time. I loved the bonding, and I nursed them all until they were a year old. Once they were able to eat solids, I felt like me again, because I could leave without feeling guilty. Those first few months were always difficult, however, because I never got to have time for myself.

Me time is so very crucial for happiness as a mom. We need that time, whether it's once a day, once a week, or even once a month to go out and be "me." It's important to not lose ourselves as we become mothers. We have to integrate our talents, gifts, and personalities into our role as mom.

What constitutes "me time?" Here are some ideas, depending on how much time you may or may not have.

- 15-30 minutes of free time:

  - hot bath (I love to throw in a yummy scented bubble bath or Lush bath bomb)
  - a walk around your neighborhood by yourself
  - lock your bedroom door and watch your favorite show uninterrupted.
  - a quick yoga or other workout video
  - wake up a little before everyone else and read a book or watch the sunrise, or maybe even both.

- 1-2 hours of free time:

  - a kid-free trip to Target (need I say more?)
  - a workout class at the local gym
  - grab some ice cream with your best friend or neighbor
  - manicure/pedicure

These are all just a few ideas of activities I like to do when I have a few minutes of free time away from my duties as a mom. Of course, these can vary greatly depending on your interests and

Mommy-Time Journal

You can jot down small mommy time activities you want to accomplish (getting your hair done, going to the movies, or reading time) to bigger me-time activities like a vacation, a concert or a nap.

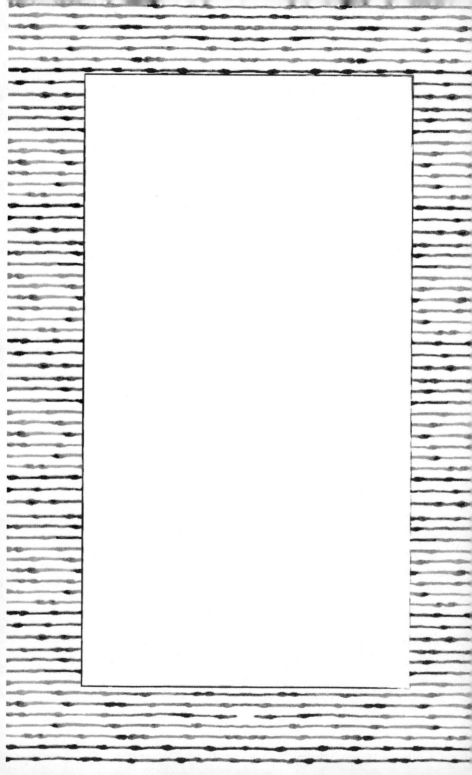

hobbies. It is most important to do something that you love. It's important to do something that will make you happy.

I know that it is not always easy to find even 5 minutes where you can be alone to do what you love. Not every woman has access to a husband, other family members, or a babysitter who can help watch the children. If that is the case and you cannot afford to actually leave your house, I suggest staying up a little later or waking up a little earlier each day. That way you can have just a few moments to yourself to collect your thoughts and organize your day.

It's not always easy to find time for ourselves. I can tell you that it is worth it, because you are worth it. We cannot take care of others if we do not first take care of ourselves.

Friends

As mentioned in a previous chapter, motherhood can be an incredibly lonely stage of life. I can tell you from personal experience that it is so much more enjoyable when you have others to share it with.

Mom friends aren't always easy to find or to make. Some people just may not be looking for

---

Here are some of my tips regarding mom friends:

---

1. Don't discount someone simply because she seems different than you. You would be surprised how much you have in common.

2. Be open in your friendships. Don't play games, and if you have something that's bothering you, be an adult and talk about it civilly. Don't let something ruin your friendship simply because you didn't dare bring it up.

3. Be prepared to make an extra effort to make mom friends. All moms are busy. It takes energy, desire, and time to plan things out. Know that all of the planning will be worth it.

4. Serve. One of the fastest ways to make friends is to show kindness and be willing to help out when needed.

5. Don't judge their parenting style. Every woman has her own way of doing things. Just because it may be different than yours doesn't make her a bad person or mother.

6. Look for mom friends who have children around the same age as you. It's a win-win for both you and your children.

7. Be complimentary. Every mom needs validation and assurance that they are doing something right. Be willing to point out the good things you see in others.

8. Be yourself. The right women will stick, and you will be able to make a strong connection.

9. Don't give up. Making mom friends won't always happen quickly. Relationships take time. If one doesn't work out, accept it and move on.

10. Be reliable. Of course life can get crazy and you will have to cancel play dates or other hang out times. But when you say you are going to be somewhere at a certain time, do it. Be someone that your friends can count on.

friendship, and others might just not like you. I can tell you, however, that it is worth going through all of the bad apples in order to get to the good one. I have had many relationships fizzle out over the years, and while I mourned some, I was relieved about others when the relationship was over.

Why are mom friends important, you might ask? Why put myself out there? You might think you are too busy and don't have the time or energy to invest into another relationship or friendship.

It is important to surround ourselves with people who are in the same situation as us. We can complain, commiserate, and understand one another. It has been one of the greatest blessings of my life to have friends who I can lean on and who validate and support me.

I know not everyone is surrounded by millions of moms who are in the same situation. As talked about in previous chapters, it's important to put yourself out there, because the reward is worth it.

Babysitters

Babysitters can be a huge blessing to all millennial moms. As I have previously mentioned, it's very important for all women to take a break once in a while. It's also important for two parents to get some alone time together and nourish their relationship without the children being present.

I live in Utah, and there are a lot of people here who have lots of family members nearby. This often comes in handy, because babysitting is free and reliable. While I have my parents living nearby, it is difficult finding time when they are available, since they both work more than full time hours.

A couple of years ago I was suffering from anxiety and depression. I had three children under the age of five, and I had little sleep and too much work to do. I suffered from major mom guilt and felt like I could never catch up. I started seeing a therapist, and the first thing she suggested was that I get some help. She told me to ask a high school girl in the neighborhood, or a friend who could swap babysitting with me. I ended up having a cute girl from the neighborhood come every Thursday afternoon for a couple of hours. Sometimes I would work, but most of the time I found myself escaping to the grocery

My Notes

store or Target. It was so fabulous to be able to go to the grocery store and be more efficient and not have to worry about tantrums or meltdowns. I felt like I could be very productive with my errands. It was also fabulous to not have to be productive too. One time I just took my two hours of free time and drove to my favorite ice cream shop. I sat there by myself and ate an ice cream cone uninterrupted. It was heaven.

In the next few months, my husband and I will have five children under the age of six. It's going to be a madhouse. I know that we are not going to get a lot of alone time as a couple, but I know that it will be very important for our relationship. Babysitting will not be cheap, but even a couple hours together as a couple sans kids once a month is very crucial for maintaining happiness in our relationship. Relationships need nurturing, and while it may be difficult, it can be possible with some effort.

Here are some of my babysitting tips for you:

1. If you can't find or afford a sitter, find a friend who you can swap babysitting with. Take turns watching each other's children so neither one of you has to pay.

2. Ask friends for any family members or sitters they know who would be willing to babysit for you.

3. Trust your gut. If you don't feel right about someone watching your children, don't let them do it. Mama instincts are real instincts.

4. If you are nervous about your babysitter putting the children down for bed (since it could be a difficult task), consider doing a day date with your spouse. We have done this numerous times, because as babies our children would not go to sleep for anyone.

5. Relax while you're away from the kids. I know it's difficult, because the babysitter may not handle everything in the exact way that you would. Most of the time it will be okay. Your kids will survive if they do not go to sleep at exactly   p.m. They will survive if the routine is not the exact same one that you have tried so hard to create. Don't sweat the small stuff and let yourself enjoy your few moments of freedom.

CHAPTER SIX

---

iMom

Technology is something that distinguishes our generation from the ones before us. As millennial moms, we have access to basically any information we need, all at our fingertips. Social media is a huge aspect of our daily lives, and as I've talked about in previous chapters, all of this technology can be harmful. In this chapter, I want to focus on the positive aspects of technology. I want to give you hope that this technology can be used for good, and that we can use it to make us happier and make things easier in our lives.

Technology And Pregnancy

Long gone are the days when women purchase 30+ books before they have their first baby. My sister once gave me 10 different books to help prepare me for my first baby back in 2010. My, how times have changed.

The wonderful thing about technology is that we can easily bring up the information we need in an app or find an answer on a search engine.

There are so many apps out there specifically designed to follow you and guide you throughout your pregnancy. These apps for your phone give you a day-by-day month-by-month way to track what size your baby is as well as fun facts and useful information. I find it fun and exciting to check my phone daily when I am pregnant to see what I can learn about my baby and what my body is doing to help create my child.

Of course there are hundreds and hundreds of pregnancy apps. Most of them are free. My advice to you would be to find an app that looks and feels like something you would want to come back to often. I am a sucker for graphic design and simplicity. I like it when there are new things and new information to learn daily. This helps make each day more exciting as I draw nearer to my due date.

It's also extremely fun to use an app with multiple pregnancies. I have found it fascinating to be able to see my progress in my current pregnancy and then be able to compare it with prior pregnancies. It's interesting to me to see how similar or how different each baby is.

I love pregnancy apps where you can keep track of photos and weight gain throughout your pregnancy. It's always great to be able to see your belly progress and see how it develops over the nine month period.

Another wonderful type of phone app during pregnancy is the apps that help keep track of your contractions. No more writing it down on a piece of paper and using a wrist watch to count how many minutes have passed in between your contractions. It is very important to track your contractions for multiple reasons. First of all, by knowing how often they are occurring, you are able to determine if you are in fact in labor. If they are close together and lasting longer, you have a good idea that you are most likely about to have your baby. Secondly, if you keep a written record of your contractions, it is perfect to be able to show your doctor and nurse. This way, they can get a good idea of where you may be in the labor process. When you call the labor and delivery unit, the first question they almost always ask is, "How far apart are your contractions?" During my last pregnancy, I used a contraction app religiously. The day I went into labor, I kept track of all of my contractions, which was very helpful when I called the hospital to tell them I thought I was actually in labor. They wanted to know how frequent my contractions were and how long they were lasting. Thanks to the app on my phone, I was able to easily give them the information they needed.

Many pregnant women have symptoms and are unfamiliar with the how, what, and why of them. Thanks to technology, we are able to Google the symptoms and get a basic idea of what could possibly be going on. Of course, if you're not careful, you can completely misdiagnose yourself, so it is definitely best to contact a nurse or doctor. It is comforting, however, to be able to research a little on your own and get a basic idea of what it is you could be experiencing.

A lot of researching is also done before women are even pregnant. Popular search terms on Google include, "how to get pregnant", "how to know when I am pregnant", and "what kinds of symptoms will I have if I am pregnant."

There are also countless online forums for women as a resource on anything pregnancy-related. Women can find all sorts of support groups on these forums and on Facebook pages. The possibilities for obtaining information are endless, and women in this generation are lucky to have access to all of it.

When I first found out that I was having twins, I had many friends approach me on Facebook. They told me that there was a specific Facebook page for women who were pregnant with multiples and who were LDS (Mormon) just like me. I was added to the group and was astonished with how many women I knew in the group. The community there is incredible. On a daily basis, there are women who are newly pregnant with multiples who have questions about symptoms, experiences with C-sections, and miscarriages. Other topics cover what baby products are best for twins, how to handle older children while handling newborn twins, etc.

This Facebook page has been a godsent for me. You can only imagine my shock and fear when I found out that my baby #4 was in fact baby #4 and baby #5. I immediately felt alone and afraid. How could I find anyone who had experienced anything similar? How was I going to get through this alone? Thank goodness for technology and for Facebook. In the last few months, I have found friendship and comfort in the Facebook community for moms of multiples. I appreciate that women share all and tell all so nothing is left to worry about. Everyone keeps it honest and real when it comes to their advice and personal experiences. Such support and openness is helpful to women like me who are trying to prepare themselves emotionally and mentally for what is to come.

How can we use technology to make pregnancy easier and better for us? Here are a few of my tips.

---

1. Download an application that speaks to you, one that you feel is easy to use and that you will look forward to each day.

2. Use your phone to document your cute pregnant belly and any symptoms you may have.

3. Join Facebook groups or online forums with women who are due around the same time as you.

4.   Download an app that can keep track of your contractions.

How can we use technology to make the postpartum stage easier for us? Here are some of my other tips:

- Download apps that help you keep track of your nursing schedule. Sometimes it can be difficult to remember what side you nursed on or for how long.

- Use applications on your phone to help you lose that baby weight. My favorite has been MyFitnessPal, as it helps document what you eat and what calories you burn each day.

- Use your phone to take pictures of your sweet newborn. You can never have enough.

- Use social media to share those pictures with your family and friends.

Technology And Relationships

Social media and the internet have caused many friendships to fail. It's true and I won't deny it. I do, however, want to focus on the positives that our modern technology brings to us as far as our relationships and friendships go. There is just as much good as bad that comes from technology. I want to dive deeper into the positive aspects of it.

Thanks to our modern age and technology, people who live across the country or world are just a FaceTime call or email away. Childhood friends and siblings who we long for and miss don't seem as far away as they used to.

My three siblings have all moved outside of Utah. It breaks my heart to its core because I miss them so. I am so grateful for the ability to call them and see them instantly. I know the same goes for many families and relationships around the world.

As a child who grew up in Saudi Arabia, I distinctly remember how big of a deal it was to call my grandparents in the United States. Not only was it expensive to call them, but we had to go to a special phone in a community center in the compound we lived in. We didn't get to talk with my grandma and grandpa very often, but it made it special when we did. I remember crying many nights because I missed them and they seemed so far away.

I am more thankful now than ever for easy, accessible ways to contact those who I love. Although they are physically far away, they are not so far away that I can't see them or communicate with them daily.

The internet has also brought people together in friendships and relationships that would not have happened otherwise. Of course there are dating websites that have helped couples find one another as well. In my case, I have been able to meet new friends from all over the world who are women just like me, trying to survive motherhood. I believe there is such power in that. The ability to bring people from different walks of life together is a powerful thing. I have found comfort, support, love, and inspiration from many different

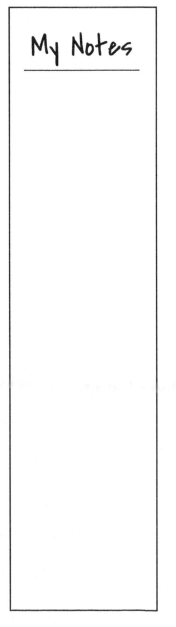

My Notes

143

women I have met online because of my YouTube channel. Some women share things with me they haven't even shared with their spouse. They feel a connection with me and I with them.

The important thing to remember is that while it wonderful to be connected to many different people at any given moment, technology cannot nurture our relationships the way we as individuals can. While it is such a great way to stay in contact with one another, it still takes effort and time to nurture a relationship outside of technology. Be wary and careful when dealing with relationships online. Not everyone is who they seem to be. Trust your gut, and be careful who you share personal information with.

So how can we take advantage of technology and use it to better our relationships? Here are some of my quick tips:

---

1. Instead of just "liking" a picture or commenting, pick up your phone and CALL someone. Catch up over the phone by talking and hearing their voice. There's nothing better for a relationship than a good old fashioned phone call.

2. Use technology to send a piece of mail. There are a few different apps now that offer the ability to take a typed message and send it to your friend, family member, etc. They will print it out and mail it for you. Receiving a piece of mail is personable and charming. It always gives me great joy to see that someone took the time to send something to me.

3. Take advantage of websites that can send gifts to your family and friends. These may include flowers, chocolate, pie, and other creative surprises. The ability to send something at the touch of a button is incredible. It's such a wonderful, easy way to let someone know you are thinking about them.

Social Media

Social media is a double edged sword. We know that those who look at it too often and spend too much time on it suffer more from depression and anxiety. We know that it causes women to compare themselves to others and that it can make people feel miserable. I also know that it can be a positive force in women's lives.

Social media is not all bad. There are many (many) positive aspects about it too. It links people and can be used as a driving force that motivates and inspires individuals to help others and be better people. I have seen funding campaigns go viral and hundreds of thousands of dollars raised to help those in need. There is power in social media, and while it can be a curse for many, for others it is a huge blessing.

The key to finding the good in social media is to find the positive in it all. I find myself drawn towards social media influencers who are positive but real about their life situations as well. I enjoy watching people who work hard and who show me that if you do so, you can be successful too. I find encouragement by following individuals who have been through difficult trials but remain calm, faithful, and happy despite it all. I find that it reminds me how to keep things in perspective and how to focus on the good in life and not just stress about things that don't mean much in the end.

One family in particular sticks out in my mind... I feel their story needs to be shared with as many people as possible because it is so powerful and inspiring.

Just a few short months ago, I found out to my surprise that instead of one baby, I was in fact having two. Instead of four children, we were going to have five, and all five of our children would be under the age of 6. My husband and I were in complete shock for a few days, and I cried for reasons good and bad. I felt overwhelmed and alone. I didn't know who I could go to for support because I didn't know anyone who had known anything similar to my situation at all. I felt hopeless.

One day I was scrolling through Instagram when I came across a local family here in Utah. They were already the parents of three children when they found out that their fourth baby was in fact triplets! Through their Instagram accounts, both husband and wife shared the difficulties and realities of having so many children. Many of the things they said resonated with me, and I felt like I had finally found someone who understood my fears.

When their triplets were almost a year old, the parents found out that one of them had a brain tumor. The family shared the progress and updates all on their social media. My heart was breaking watching it all unfold. I felt like I just wanted to jump through my phone and support the family and give them all of the support and love I could.

Here are some tips on how you can use social media to better yourself and others:

1. Follow accounts that uplift, inspire, and motivate you. Don't spend your time on negative sites or social media influencers who bring you down.

2. Post uplifting, encouraging content. Share the good things, and keep it real but positive. You never know who will stumble across your social media account and need the extra boost.

3. Spread the word whenever possible. If you find an inspirational person or situation where someone you care about needs help, don't be afraid to share it with your friends and contacts. I truly believe that what goes around comes around, and sharing goodness will only lead to goodness in your personal life.

Sadly, just a few days ago in December their little boy passed away due to the cancer.

Although I didn't know the family personally, I cried many tears. I have been in awe at their faith, positive attitudes, and calm demeanor. I have been amazed at how the online community has embraced and supported their family. Tens of thousands of people have messaged and commented on all of their posts stating that they are praying for them and that they want to help in some way.

Social media can be a power for good. I have seen that especially with regard to the incredible family

I mentioned above. Each day, I am reminded by their pictures and posts that life is precious and that we should all take time to enjoy the little moments we have with our children and loved ones. I am grateful that they are so willing to share their experiences with their followers, because they exemplify happiness amidst sorrow and pain. It motivates me to be the same in my personal life.

All in all, technology does not have to be a negative, scary thing. As millennial moms, we can use the tools we have at our fingertips to uplift and better ourselves. Make sure to keep that in mind as you seek out advice and social media influencers to follow. Social media can be powerful in a good way. It takes filtering out the negativity to reap the benefits that technology can bring.

My Notes

CHAPTER SEVEN

Pamper Yourself

I f there is one thing that you take away from this book let it be this; it's important to TREAT YOURSELF. Amidst the chaos that is motherhood and trying to figure out who you are now that you have a child, it's okay to take time for yourself. It's okay to do things that you loved to do before having children. It's all right to take a breather and do something nice to spoil yourself.

You might be reading this and thinking, "Michelle, you're crazy. How would I ever find time for myself when I have so much on my plate?" Well, let it be known that it is not always easy. However, I can tell you how important it truly is to take a mommy time out once in a while. It might seem impossible given your situation. Maybe you are single and maybe you have no access to babysitters or family. Whatever it is that you have to do, work hard and make it happen.

Last year, I wanted to take a weekend off in Park City, Utah, along with six of my close girlfriends. We would only be gone for two days and one night. We planned to just relax, spend time at the spa and go out to eat at a nice restaurant. Between the seven of us, it took lots of planning to make sure we could all get sitters and husbands on board. With a lot of rearranging schedules, we all made it happen. We spent those two days relaxing and enjoying some girl time. Worth every second.

A couple of years ago, my husband Brad and I won a trip through his work to spend a few days in Las Vegas. It was all expenses paid including hotel and car. It sounded like a perfect getaway for the two of us. The tricky part was going to be finding someone who could take care of our kids. Thankfully, I have incredible friends who made it all possible. Each day we were gone, I had a different friend watch the kids, and Brad's younger sister was able to take care of them and sleep over at our house at night. I remember scheduling the whole trip for my friends and sister-in-law. It was very complicated, but thankfully it worked, and Brad and I were able to enjoy a relaxing few days sans kids.

Why is it so important to take time to treat ourselves as mothers? I honestly feel like I could write an entire book on that topic alone. It's important for our sanity, our happiness, and our well-being. There's no way we can even imagine taking care of others if we do not first take care of ourselves. If we are drowning, there is no way we can save or help someone else. We must be afloat on our own in order to be able to help others around us survive. So it is with motherhood.

Most mothers tend to put themselves last on every priority list. Their children, spouses, and friends usually take importance over them. The demands of motherhood are endless. Mothers are expected to provide emotional and physical support for so many on a daily basis. We are expected to be on time to appointments and to always have a clean house and a hot body. We are supposed to teach our children manners, math, and social cues. So many things on all of our plates.

There have been many nights when I have been up all night with a sick baby or two and my mind was racing a million miles an hour. I couldn't stop thinking about all of the expectations on me and the places I had to be the next day. I thought about how exhausted I would be, and all of that stressed me out.

Take comfort in knowing that if you have ever had those feelings you are truly not alone. Every mother, I don't care where you come from or what your background is, has at one point or another felt like they didn't know what they were doing.

How do we keep ourselves sane? How do we feel happy and productive when we are being pulled in so many directions at once? Remember always that it's important to TREAT YOURSELF.

I find it funny and kind of ironic that I am writing this chapter at this point in my life. I am currently 23 weeks pregnant with my twin girls. I have three other children (6 yrs., 4 yrs., and 20 months) that I attempt to take care of every day. I find it difficult to walk, let alone bend over. It's a workout to simply walk up the stairs. I don't have any help from family, and I find myself working late and during any free moment I get. I feel judged on a daily basis on my social media, because either I don't feed my children healthy food, or my house isn't spotless all of the time. The pressure is real.

I can tell you though that I've never been happier in my life. I find time each and every day to have a few moments to myself. I can't afford to have a nanny or cleaning lady help me with my daily tasks, but I can afford to take 15 minutes to myself at the end of the day for a nice hot bubble bath. When I'm not pregnant, I wait for my husband to get home from work, and the second he walks in the door, I have my running clothes on and I head out on a nice evening run.

I challenge you to do the same. Find a time once a day or once a week where you can take care of you. I know that each woman has their ideal moment of peace. I encourage you to brainstorm and list ways that you can find time to relax and take care of yourself.

One of my neighbor friends set up a wonderful mommy

My Notes
_____

155

relaxation day for us tomorrow. I don't know if I'll be able to sleep, I'm so excited. She has arranged for a sitter to watch our kids and a massage therapist to come to her house and give us all massages. She has prepared food and treats so we can have just a couple of hours of good relaxation time. It truly sounds like a dream.

Of course, activities like that are not accessible to everyone. It's the first time anything like that has happened to me in my six and a half years of motherhood. In order to pamper ourselves, we do not always have to go all out, however. A lot of taking care of ourselves comes in the small and simple things that we can do for ourselves each and every day.

I find that it's important to take care of ourselves physically, emotionally, and socially as mothers. While it may seem like a lot of work and effort, I can promise you that it is worth it in the long run.

Here are some of my tips on how you can pamper yourself both in big and small ways:

1. Always wash your face and brush your teeth each and every morning.

2. Find your signature scent. On days when you feel down or exhausted, spray your favorite perfume or use your favorite lotion. Doing something small like that can lift your mood.

3. Take a hot bath. Use bath bombs, bath salts, and/or bubble bath. Light candles around the tub and listen to your favorite music.

4. Go get a pedicure. Find a place near to you, call up a girlfriend and enjoy an hour of relaxation.

5. Buy yourself some fresh flowers. (I love the ones they sell at Costco. They are usually a great price and are beautiful.)

6. Buy your favorite treat and eat it while you watch a chick flick or binge watch your favorite show.

7. Do yoga. Find a local gym that has a class, or find a class online that you can do.

8. Plan a girls' night out with family or friends.

9. Go on a run or walk around your neighborhood.

10. Get a facial at a salon or do one at home. Sheet masks have become one of my favorite things to do at home when I want to pamper myself.

11. Get your hair done at a salon. Try getting just a blow out too.

Tip: Look for local beauty schools in your area. Most places offer discounted facials, massages and hair styling.

Now that I have given you some ideas I would like for you to sit for a minute and think of 10 different ways you could treat and pamper yourself throughout your day and week.

Five Ways I can Take Care of Myself on a Daily Basis:

-
-
-
-
-

Five Ways I can Take Care of Myself on a Weekly Basis:

-
-
-
-
-

The Importance Of Being Selfish

A normal day for a mother consists of feeding, bathing, comforting, and entertaining their little ones. A mother's schedule frequently revolves around the nap schedule of her baby. While it is obviously important to tend to the needs of our children, it's also important to take some time to be selfish.

Mothers are constantly pulled in many directions. We are expected to be places and to please other people. Whether it's work-related, school-related, or social obligations, it is easy for a woman to feel overwhelmed.

I'm going to share with you some advice that changed my mom life. A therapist once told me how important it was to create boundaries in my life. She told me that at times it could possibly hurt someone's feelings or change a relationship that I had with someone, but she emphasized how important it was to set boundaries and make rules.

I don't know about you, but I have always been a people pleaser. I am scared to offend and especially scared to say 'no.' Throughout my life, I have had instances where I felt like someone was walking all over me and I couldn't voice my opinion or do what I really wanted to do simply because I didn't want to hurt someone's feelings and cause any sort of drama.

I started seeing a therapist when I was pregnant with my third child. I was overwhelmed with life. I was at a breaking point, and my anxiety was at an all-time high. I knew that I needed professional help if I wanted to feel better living my life. I felt like I was always having to do what other people wanted me to do. I felt like I had no voice and that I was constantly doing things just to please people, not because I sincerely wanted to do them. The minute I started to say 'no', everything changed for the better. Sure, I lost a couple of friends along the way, but I felt empowered because I no longer belonged to someone else and I didn't have to explain myself to anyone.

It is important for you as a young mom to realize this from the beginning of your motherhood experience. Throughout your time as a mom, you will be pulled in many directions. You will feel like you have to do it all and do it all well. You will want to please your

My Notes

children, your family, your neighbors, and your acquaintances.

If you feel like a family event is going to interfere with your baby's nap time, it's okay to say 'no' and not attend. It's okay to not be available for a party because you've been up all night with your baby. There will be countless situations where you will feel obligated to do something you don't want to do.

Of course it's important to take into account other people's feelings. But please (please) remember to include yourself and your feelings too. It's important to be selfish once in a while.

One common situation that comes to mind is the holiday season. Of course it's wonderful to surround ourselves with our family and other important people in our lives; especially during the holidays. Once you add children into the equation, everything changes, and what once was a simple trip to see family is now more expensive and more stressful.

One thing that my husband Brad and I decided to do was to always be home for Christmas. We wanted that consistency for our children. We wanted to avoid traveling during the holidays as we wanted to be able to relax instead of traveling during the busy season. While it has been hard at times to be away from family during such a special time of year, it has been such a wonderful thing for our little family. Brad and I have been able to make traditions for our children, and we have been able to fully relax and enjoy our home with our kids during the holiday season.

I want you to take a minute and think of a few things in your life that you need to be more selfish about. Take a few minutes to think about the following questions and answer them accordingly.

Are there any relationships in your life that you feel are unbalanced?

Do you feel like you know someone who constantly tells you what to do?

When was the last time you did something that you wanted to do?

How often do you do something because you feel obligated to and not because you sincerely want to?

When was the last time you said "no" to someone?

Of course, it's important in life to help other people and maintain good relationships. I'm definitely not implying that you should burn bridges and ruin relationships. I want you to take away the fact it is important to factor in your feelings and voice early on so that you can be the wife, mother, friend, etc. that you want to be.

Your time is precious, and you need to put energy and effort into happy, positive relationships. Life is too short to waste on people who make you feel worse or who bring you down. One of the hardest things I've had to do is to move on from those types of relationships in my life. After it was all said and done, I can say that cutting out those toxic, negative relationships has made me happier than ever. I feel free, and I feel like I am able to

be a better wife and mother because I don't have negativity and bad relationships weighing me down. It feels great to give my children the best of me. My time is precious, and I want to spend it with those that I love the most.

Taking Time For Your Spouse

Just as it is important to care of yourself as a mother, it is also important to take care of your relationship with your spouse. As I'm sure you have noticed now that you have a little one, this can be difficult for a multitude of reasons.

I remember clearly how having our first baby changed everything in our lives. Our time together as husband and wife was a lot more limited. What we used to spend on dates and trips now went to diapers and baby food. Just as any relationship needs nurturing, our relationships with our significant others do too.

As new parents, my husband and I found it extremely hard to find time for one another. Our baby would not take a bottle, so it was difficult to leave him with a baby sitter. We were both tired from the late nights and lack of sleep. We were in survival mode, and the last thing we could imagine was taking time away from our baby.

It wasn't until we had been parents for three years that we were offered a trip through my husband's work to Cabo San Lucas, Mexico. It

My Notes

was a work trip that my husband had earned, and it was an all-expense-paid trip. For an average person, the idea of such a trip would be mind-blowing. An all-expense-paid trip to Mexico, who would turn something like that down?

When I found about the trip, I was excited. Well, kind of. I knew that this was my opportunity to be selfish about my relationship with my husband. There was no way we would turn down such an incredible vacation. I of course worried about my two little boys, who were only one and three at the time. I was scared that it would be difficult for them if my husband and I left them for five days and four nights. Thankfully, everything went perfectly fine. The kids had a couple of sad moments while we were gone, but that was to be expected.

We came home feeling closer to each other as parents and feeling more appreciation for our children because we had missed them while we were gone.

Don't forget that your relationship as parents is important, because parenting is all about teamwork. It's important to help each other share the load. When one person is lacking, it's important to step up and help out when you can. Spending alone time together as parents is critical because it keeps the bond between you strong and healthy.

There have been many moments as a mother where I felt like I had nothing more to give. I was tired, emotionally drained, and at my wit's end. I cannot express enough gratitude for my sweet husband and for all of those times when he stepped in when I couldn't take anymore. For better or for worse, in sickness and in health. Parenting is all about teamwork, and I know a team approach is imperative to keep our relationship happy and healthy and keep us feeling like we are partners.

I know that being selfish goes against what we have been taught since we were children. I know that it's difficult to change that mindset. I think that it's important to remember that while it's not good to be selfish all of the time, it is important to be selfish some of the time. We need to do what we can to keep ourselves happy so we can keep others happy as well.

CHAPTER EIGHT

My Favorite Recipes For The Millennial Mom

I am currently writing this chapter on my laptop at my OBGYN's office. I am sitting in a very uncomfortable chair, and the laptop is resting on my lap. My arms are stretched as far as they can go as I type, because my pregnant belly is large and doesn't make much room for my laptop. I am quite the picture right now. I am currently taking the glucose or gestational diabetes test. I just had to drink a very (very) sugary fruit punch drink, and now I wait for an hour for the doctor's staff to see about my blood sugar levels. Since I had to do this test today, I have been restricted on what I have been able to eat for the last 12 hours. I was told no sugar, no fruits (because they have sugar), no bread, basically everything I normally eat.

I find it very fitting that today I get to write to you about some of my favorite go-to recipes. I am in no way a professional cook, but I consider myself a pro at eating and enjoying food. I feel like I have a good sense of what tastes good and what my children will also eat. Thanks to the magic of our internet age, I have been able to test hundreds and hundreds of recipes throughout my mom life; and I have gathered some of my favorite recipes, and some of my close girlfriends' recipes, to share with you at the end of this chapter. Stay tuned because they are yummy!

Millennial mom life is a fast-paced life. We have millions of places to be at any given moment. Balance is key when it comes to all aspects of motherhood. As you know, as mothers we are expected to do it all and to do it all perfectly. Not only are our houses supposed to look Pinterest worthy and Instagram chic, but our kids must always be clean and dressed in the latest trendy outfit. We also are supposed to work out often and cook perfectly healthy meals for the members of our family. There is lots of pressure from society to do it all and do it all well. Social media sets the standards of our society today. Because of it, we are shown what the "ideal" life is and what it should look like. We are rarely shown real life but mostly shown what we should try to obtain instead.

If you're anything like me, you have been struggling to survive. With a newborn, you're struggling to feed the baby as well as perhaps take care of other children and keep the house from burning down. The idea of a shower seems impossible, and your idea of getting ready is changing your sweats into other less dirty sweats and brushing your teeth. Your whole day's goal is simply to survive until your significant other walks through the door. I cannot tell you how many times my husband has come home from work to find that I haven't had anything to eat for the day. It is sad and scary, but true. There have been days where I have found myself so busy taking care of my children that sometimes I forget to feed myself.

Mothers obviously need to take care of themselves and feed themselves too. Just as with exercise, mothers need to take time to care for their health and eat the right foods. When you are putting the right foods and nutrients into your body, you will feel better and your body will be better able to take care of your baby and family. (Says the lady who loves cookies and diet coke when it's been a rough day.)

I want you to know that as I write this book I find myself stopping and chuckling multiple times. Not because I think I am funny, but because I feel like I am telling all of you the advice that sometimes I need to hear myself.

As you are probably aware by this point in the book, my first pregnancy was a rough one. Not only was it difficult for me because we were poor young college students, but also because I gained the most weight, 70 pounds to be exact. I was large and in charge and was more uncomfortable than I could have ever imagined. After I had my son Will, I was determined to lose all of the weight.

I worked hard and ended up 15 pounds lighter than before I had my baby boy. Let me tell you how.

I started to work out two to three times a week. It was over six years ago, when Zumba was the huge new craze. I loved dancing and having a blast, all while burning lots of calories. While I definitely know that working out was a big part of my weight loss, I know that the majority of my weight loss was due to changing what I ate.

We did not have a lot of money at the time and were living in my Brad's grandfather's basement apartment. We counted every penny that came into and went out of our bank account. Because of this, we were very (very) good about preparing our own healthy meals from home. We rarely went out to eat, and that helped us save money and calories. I planned every meal ahead of time and was able to

My Notes

My Notes

be efficient about what I needed to buy at the grocery store. It made a big difference for our health and bank account.

My husband and I both dropped the pounds quickly. We had never been healthier in our entire lives. I felt revitalized; I knew everything that I was putting into my body, and it gave me the energy that I needed to take care of my newborn baby boy. We were eating healthy and so was he. He grew to love fruits and vegetables, and to this day he is not a picky eater. Both when he was a growing baby and then once he became a toddler, we were active as a family. We would go on family hikes, runs, and walks. Eating healthy and living an active lifestyle became our family norm.

When I was pregnant with my second boy, Max, I gained about 40 pounds total. Then I had the same postpartum goal to lose weight and be my healthiest. I decided to count my calories and watch everything that I put into my body. I really enjoyed using the app "MyFitnessPal" on my phone to help me keep track of what I was putting into my body. I know that there are lots of similar apps and ways to keep track, but I really enjoyed having the information all right there on my phone. I loved that I could put in what I had eaten and what exercise I had done. It made it easier for me to see and count my calories eaten and calories burned. Being accountable helped me get into the best shape of my life. I was able to train for my first triathlon and first half marathon. I attribute it all to putting the right food and the right amount of food into my body.

Throughout my life, I have noticed that even if I worked out multiple times a week, my shape never really changed if I didn't change my diet. Food is such an important part of our health, and finding good balanced meals can be hard for the busy mom.

I wish I could say that we eat that same way in our family today. Sometimes we do and sometimes we don't. Life, pregnancy, and children get in the way. I have a goal this year to get back into the same meal planning that I did back then after I have my babies in the next couple of months.

Before I share with you some of my best recipes, I wanted to share with you some tips on how you can plan your meals. Meal planning saves you time and money and makes mealtime less stressful for everyone.

---

1. Once a week (I prefer Sunday evening), sit down with your planner and favorite recipes. Take a look at what your schedule in the upcoming week is. This helps determine when you will have time to prep meals and when you will have to have something quick and easy.

2. Once you know your schedule for the week, pick out which recipes will work best on which day.

3. When you have decided what meals you want to prepare, write out a list of what ingredients you will need for your meals. Create a shopping list.

4. Monday morning, head to the grocery store and get the items on your list.

5. Enjoy a week where you don't have to worry about what you can come up with for dinner. Everything will be planned and purchased, so all you have to do is prepare it.

Recipes

I am beyond excited to share with you some of my favorite go-to meals. Some of them are healthier than others, but I promise you they are all delicious. I have collected my favorites and have asked my closest friends (aka my Gem Jam ladies) to share with you some of their favorites as well!

The first dish I wanted to share with you comes from the beautiful Tanya Rasmussen. She's one of the most athletic people I know and has a killer six-pack. She travels the world with her husband on a regular basis, and her son is my little girl Molly's boyfriend. :) She has made dinner for us countless times when we have been under the weather, and this is one of her go-tos! Enjoy!

1.

Slow Cooker Chicken Marsala

Prep Time:

10Minutes

Cook Time:

6 hours;

Serves:

4

Ingredients:

- 4 boneless skinless chicken breasts
- salt and pepper to taste (I used about ½ teaspoon of each)
- 2 teaspoons minced garlic
- 1 cup sliced mushrooms
- 1 cup sweet marsala cooking wine (may sub chicken broth in a pinch)
- ½ cup water
- ¼ cup cornstarch
- fresh parsley, roughly chopped

Instructions:

Lightly grease your slow cooker with nonstick spray. Season chicken with salt and pepper and place in the bottom of your slow cooker. Top chicken with garlic, mushrooms, and marsala wine. Cover and cook for five to six hours on low. Use a slotted spoon to transfer chicken to a plate. Whisk together water and cornstarch until dissolved, then pour into slow cooker and stir. Add chicken back to slow cooker, switch heat to high, cover and cook another 20-30 minutes until sauce is thickened. Taste and add salt and pepper as needed. Sprinkle with parsley and serve. Recipe by Creme De La Crumb at http://www.lecremedelacrumb.com/slow-cooker-chicken-marsala/

2.

The Best Mashed Potatoes Ever

(Tanya likes to serve this as a side dish with the Chicken Marsala dish.)

Cook Time:

15 Minutes

Ingredients:

- 4 pounds Russet Potatoes, peeled and chopped into two or so inch pieces
- 1/2 cup (1 stick) Butter
- 8 oz. (1 block) Cream Cheese
- 1/4 cup Grated Parmesan Cheese
- 1 cup Sour Cream (or Greek Yogurt)
- 1/4 cup Half & Half
- Salt
- water

Instructions:

Add the potatoes to a large pot and add enough water to cover them. Salt the water liberally and bring the water to a boil.

While the potatoes are cooking, quarter the butter and cream cheese, then add them and the cheese, sour cream and heavy cream to a large mixing bowl.

When the potatoes are tender (15-20 minutes), drain well and add them while still hot to the mixing bowl. Whip until smooth. I prefer to use my KitchenAid stand mixer with the whisk attachment.

If the potatoes are too thick, slowly add more half and half (or milk) until they reach the desired consistency.

3.

Peanut Ginger Chicken And Mango Salsa

This next recipe comes from another one of my gorgeous Gem Jam friends. Her name is Julie Sistrunk, and she is as kind as she is beautiful. She has a heart of gold and serves others constantly. I don't know where I would be without her! She is humble and doesn't like a lot of attention. I was so excited to include her in this book to give her some of the recognition she deserves. Love her like a sister!

This recipe is one of my favorites that she makes! It's fresh and flavorful. It definitely requires more preparation time, but the results are fantastic, and my husband and kids love it as well!

Step #1: Marinate the chicken.

Marinade:

- ½ cup boiling water
- ½ cup creamy peanut butter
- ¼ cup bottled chili garlic sauce (Found in the Asian food aisle)
- 3 Tbsp. soy sauce
- 2 Tbsp. vegetable oil
- 2 Tbsp. vinegar
- 1 Tbsp. ground ginger
- 4-8 chicken breasts

Instructions:

Cut chicken breasts into strips and place into zip lock bag.

Boil water and stir in peanut butter. The mixture will first get stiff but then will soften.

Stir in chili sauce, oil, soy sauce, vinegar and ginger. Pour mixture over chicken inside zip lock bag.

Make sure that chicken is coated in marinade and chill in refrigerator overnight or minimum one hour.

Mango Salsa:

- 2 cups chopped mangos (Frozen mangos work as well)
- 1 chopped cucumber
- ½ cup Chopped cilantro
- 3 ½ tbsp. Sugar
- 1 Tbsp. vegetable oil
- 1 Tbsp. vinegar

Instructions:

In a medium sized bowl combine mango, cucumber, cilantro, sugar, oil, and vinegar. Cover and chill in refrigerator until serving.

Coconut Rice

- 2 Cups coconut milk
- 2 cups water
- 2 cups white rice
- 3 ½ Tbsp. sugar
- ½ tsp. Salt

Instructions:

Combine all ingredients for rice in a rice cooker and press start. It should take approximately 15-20 minutes to cook.

If you don't have a rice cooker, combine all ingredients in a saucepan and bring to a boil. Stir once and cover, turning heat to simmer. Let cook 18-20 minutes or until rice is tender and liquid is gone.

Chicken Breasts
Instructions:

After the chicken has marinated, cook the chicken. We have found that grilling is best. We especially love using the indoor George Foreman grill. You can also just broil it in the oven or else fry in a pan until done.

4.

The Best Buttermilk Pancakes Ever!

When I lived in Ukraine for 18 months as a missionary, I made these buttermilk pancakes all of the time. It was a taste of home for me and my fellow missionaries. It's simple and doesn't require any difficult ingredients. It's become a staple for Saturday mornings here at the Pearson home. It's also best served with homemade buttermilk syrup.

Ingredients:

- 2 eggs
- 2 cups buttermilk
- 4 Tbsp. oil
- 2 cups flour
- 2 Tbsp. sugar
- 2 tsp. baking powder
- 2 tsp. baking soda
- ½ tsp. salt

Instructions:

Beat the eggs and add the other ingredients in the order given. Mix until smooth. Grease heated skillet. Pour batter from the tip of large spoon or from pitcher onto hot skillet. Turn pancakes as soon as they are puffed and full of bubbles but before bubbles break. Bake on other side until golden brown.

5.

The Best Buttermilk Syrup Recipe (Aka Magic Sauce)

Ingredients:

- 1 cube butter (½ cup)
- ¾ cup sugar
- ½ cup buttermilk
- 1 tsp. baking soda
- 1 tsp. vanilla

Instructions:

Over medium heat, melt the butter and sugar. Once the butter is melted, add the buttermilk. Stir mixture until it begins to boil, and then remove from heat. Stir in the baking soda and the vanilla.

Make sure that you do it in a bigger pan than you think that you will need. The baking soda makes it foam up pretty high when you first put it in. This syrup is excellent on pancakes, French toast, and crepes.

6.

Easy Apricot Chicken

This recipe is taken from one of my all-time favorite cookbooks, which is no longer in print (the Keeping Up Cookbook). It is my go-to meal when I need to whip up a delicious dinner for my family or for friends. It's a favorite of anyone I have prepared it for.

Ingredients:

- 4 boncless skinless chicken breasts
- ½ cup apricot jam
- 1 ½ tablespoons soy sauce
- 1 tablespoon prepared whole grain mustard
- 1 tablespoon butter
- ¼ cup sliced almonds

Instructions:

Pat chicken breasts dry and season with salt and pepper, then place in a greased 9 x 13 baking dish. Bake for 10 minutes in a 400 degree oven.

Meanwhile, stir together remaining ingredients (except almonds) in a saucepan. Heat until well combined, stirring often. Pour sauce over chicken and continue to bake for 10 to 15 minutes or until chicken is cooked through. Sprinkle chicken with almonds, and briefly broil until almonds toast and sauce begins to caramelize.

I love to serve this chicken with a side of chicken flavored Rice-A-Roni and some roasted broccoli. It makes for a flavorful, filling dinner.

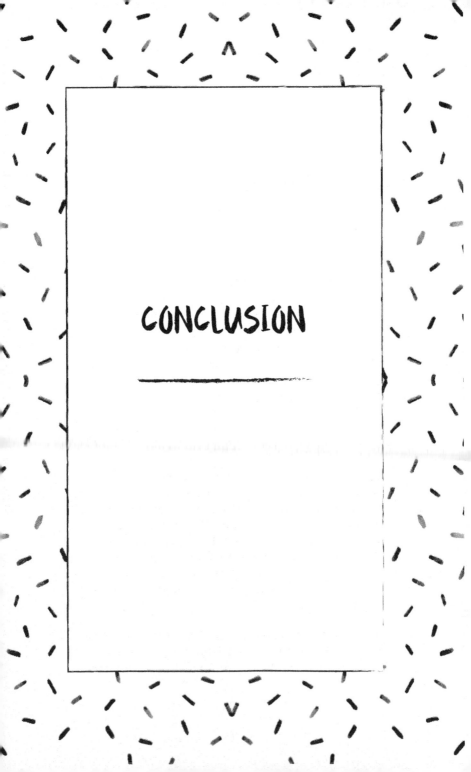

CONCLUSION

So there you have it. I have done my very best at compiling all of the advice I wish I had known as a new mother. I hope you have been able to learn and feel more confident as you approach this new stage of life. I am excited for you. I know that you can do it. There will be hard days, and there will be nights where you feel like you are going crazy. You will be more tired than you ever thought was humanly possible. Just know that it will all be worth it. Every single second will be worth it, and you will most likely want to do it all over again.

I am excited for you to experience one of the most incredible days of your life, the day that you will become a mother. I always tell my family and friends that the day I go into labor is always one of the best days of my life. I feel just as excited as I did on my wedding day. Of course, labor itself may not be a cakewalk for everyone, but just know that the prize will be worth more than you could ever possibly imagine.

Writing this book has been a very therapeutic process for me. I have written it during some of the most stressful mom moments of my life to date. I have battled twin pregnancy while having gallbladder issues. (Maybe TMI but just keeping it real.) I've been trying my best to take care of my three other children while at the same time trying to keep up with my YouTube channel and writing this book. I tell you this not to brag, but to show you that it can all be done. If I can do it, you better believe you can too. Anything you desire as a mother can be accomplished. It may be stressful, and you may reach your breaking point, but as long as you take care of yourself first, you can take care of your children and pursue your dreams too.

If you take anything away from this book, I hope it is that you need to always trust your gut. You will get recommendations from everyone around you. Friends, sisters, and complete strangers will tell you that you are doing things incorrectly. Take it all with a grain of salt and know that nobody knows your child better than you do. Know that it's okay to do things differently than others, and that just because you may be different in the way you approach a certain technique, that does not make you a bad mother. Trust in yourself and in your instincts. You will have it all down before you know it.

There will be times when you will get caught up on the next stage. You will find yourself saying, "I can't wait until my baby is that old" or "Once my baby is that old I will..." Make sure that you stop yourself from doing that, and don't get too caught up in the future. Enjoy every moment that you can, because before you know it your little newborn will be leaving for their first day of kindergarten. When you are up late at night soothing a crying baby, take a moment to soak it all in. Cherish the moments when your baby needs you and that their biggest problem is that they need a clean diaper. Take the time to put your phone away and choose to be present with your baby. Smell them, hold them, and play with them. Enjoy the days when you have nowhere to be and nothing to do. Before you know it, they will have soccer practice and play dates and a million other places to be besides with you.

Know that it's okay to make mistakes. Know that everything you try may not work for you and your baby like it does for someone else. No technique works on every single baby 100% of the time. Trust me. Be okay with that. Take comfort that no mother is perfect, no matter how much she may appear to have it all together. We are all trying to figure this whole motherhood thing out. Some of us just hide it better than others.

Also know that you are never alone. There is always someone going through something similar and at the same stage of life as you. Try to find your tribe that can support and uplift you on the hard days. Be there for them like you want them to be there for you. Don't be afraid to get out of your comfort zone and find those women and relationships that every woman needs and desires. Know that rejection is real and that some people are meant to be in our lives for just a short period of time.

Take time for yourself. Don't get so caught up in routines or schedules that you forget to make time to take a step back and breathe. Take a hot bath. Go on a long run. Go get a massage or go to dinner with a friend. Make sure you are also taking care of you. Spoil yourself, and don't feel guilty about it. Pursue your dreams. Don't let your title of "mom" stop you from doing what you've always wanted to do. Of course having children makes it more difficult, but don't ever give up. Remember that you are a person too, and that you must continue to cultivate your talents and mind.

Forgive yourself. There will be times when you are short-tempered and have little patience. You might say something to your spouse or to your child that you may regret. Know that it's okay to make mistakes, because it only means you are one step closer to becoming the mother you want to become. Make it a priority to let go of mistakes and move on. Apologize when you need to, but always move on. The last thing you need as a mom is excess baggage of things that you can't change.

Mom guilt is a real thing. You will never be able to do everything for your child like you want to. You will always be able to find something that you aren't doing well enough. Know that this is completely normal. It's important to remember that your child won't remember everything you do incorrectly. They will only remember how they felt and if they felt loved.

Stop comparing yourself to others. "Comparison is the thief of joy." Any time you find yourself wishing you had what someone else has or comparing someone's house, style, or weight to your own: STOP IT. No matter how perfect their life may seem, know that it isn't. Every mother and every woman has a battle that they are fighting. Some are more clear to be seen, while others are secrets that nobody will ever know.

Make sure to write things down. Write in a journal, or document with photographs. Even though it may seem like you'll never forget your labor or the first steps your baby takes, trust me, you will forget a lot of the details. I find so much joy going back and reading in my journal how I felt in those very moments. They come and go so quickly that the only way to remember them is to check back on what I've recorded.

Get excited for the incredible opportunity to be someone's mother. I cannot express to you the joy I feel when my babies first utter the word "mama." There is something so special about having a little innocent baby desire to be loved and cared for by you. There is a sense of importance and love that you will never experience in any other way. The bond is real and the connection strong. There is a sense of power knowing that your child has different cries when they want different things. There is a sense of accomplishment when you are able to calm your crying child simply by picking them up. There is so much happiness that comes with watching your child enter new stages and accomplish new tasks; learning to walk, learning to talk, learning to read. It's all so wonderful, and you are just about to embark on that journey.

As you know, motherhood is not going to be the easiest thing you have done. You will cry tears of joy and tears of discouragement and exhaustion. The key is to never give up and to continue to do your best. Take time to take deep breaths, and know that a bad day/bad month/bad year does not mean a bad life. Motherhood is not a nine to five job, and you will be more emotionally, mentally, and physically tired than you have ever been in your life. You will be stretched beyond measure. You will find that you will be able to love in a way that you never have before.

Motherhood is unlike anything you have ever experienced. You will change in ways that you never thought possible. Get ready for the best job you will ever have.

Motherhood has been the greatest honor of my life. I cherish my children and would give anything to see them successful and happy. I have learned so much about myself and I know I will grow and stretch a lot more in the future too. My children have helped me become a better person and have shown me what true love and unconditional love are all about.

Thank you for taking the time to read this book. I hope you found it helpful and informative. I hope that you have found comfort in its pages and that it has made you realize your potential as a future mother.

I believe in you. You can do this. The days may seem long, and you may feel like you don't know what you're doing, but just know that you will figure it out. Remember to take a deep breath and get ready for the most rewarding time of your life.

AUTHOR

Michelle Pearson is a mommy to 5 children ages 6 and under. She has been on Youtube since early 2011 and has enjoyed sharing her love for motherhood with women from different places and walks of life. Michelle has lived all over the world and is fluent in Thai and Russian. She enjoys running, singing, playing the piano, eating and most importantly spending time with her husband and beautiful children. Motherhood is no easy task but Michelle is thankful every day for the opportunity to be a mother and considers it her "dream job."

Publisher's Note

Thank you for reading.

In writing *Deep Breaths*, Michelle Pearson did her very best to produce the most accurate, well-written and mistake-free book. Yet, as with all things human (and certainly with books), mistakes are inevitable. Despite Michelle's and the publisher's best efforts at proofreading and editing, some number of errors will emerge as the book is read by more and more people.

We ask for your help in producing a more perfect book by sending us any errors you discover at errata@mango.bz or to the author at michellepearsonyt@gmail.com. We will strive to correct these errors in future editions of this book. Thank you in advance for your help.

CPSIA information can be obtained
at www.ICGtesting.com
Printed in the USA
BVOW10s1129190717
489734BV00002B/2/P